THEDA♡CARE
CENTER FOR
HEALTHCARE VALUE

Targeting Value, Spreading Change

Other titles available from

THEDA♡CARE
CENTER FOR
HEALTHCARE VALUE

On the Mend: Revolutionizing Healthcare
to Save Lives and Transform the Industry
by John Toussaint, MD
and Roger A. Gerard, Phd

Potent Medicine:
The Collaborative Cure for Healthcare
by John Toussaint, MD
with Emily Adams

Beyond Heroes:
A Lean Management System for Healthcare
by Kim Barnas
with Emily Adams

Management on the Mend:
The Healthcare Executive Guide to System Transformation

by John Toussaint, MD

with Emily Adams

THEDA♡CARE
CENTER FOR
HEALTHCARE VALUE
Appleton, WI

THEDA♡CARE
CENTER FOR
HEALTHCARE VALUE
Targeting Value, Spreading Change

ThedaCare Center for Healthcare Value
100 W. Lawrence Street
Appleton, WI 54911 USA
createvalue.org

Publisher's Cataloging-in-Publication Data
Toussaint, John.

Management on the mend : the healthcare executive guide to system transformation / John Toussaint, with Emily Adams. – Appleton, WI : ThedaCare Center for Healthcare Value, 2015.

p. ; cm.

ISBN13: 978-0-9848848-5-8

1. Health services administration--United States. 2. Health care reform--United States. 3. Organizational behavior. I. Title. II. Adams, Emily.

RA395.A3 T687 2015

362.10973—dc23   2015934602

Project coordination by Jenkins Group, Inc.
www.BookPublishing.com

Interior layout by Brooke Camfield

Printed in the United States of America

19   18   17   16   15   •   5   4   3   2   1

FSC
www.fsc.org
MIX
Paper from
responsible sources
FSC® C002589

All Tish wanted was a little less winter. The cold Midwest was hard on her scoliosis and arthritis plagued her nights. Sleeping pills helped some, but what she really needed was sunshine and warm, balmy nights. So she and her husband of more than half a century, Ted, went south.

A few weeks into their stay in a Florida condo, Tish started coughing. She coughed so long and hard she was nauseous and feared pneumonia. At the immediate-care clinic, a doctor prescribed an antibacterial drug and steroids for what was probably a nanovirus[1] and told Ted to take her home to rest. But Tish could not keep the pills down and her coughing got worse. They called the doctor, but he never called back.

Three days later, Tish was in an emergency room, severely dehydrated. Then she was admitted to a medical unit where she developed a urinary tract infection, was repeatedly stuck with a needle, and was ignored when she complained about a skin tear above her elbow. In 48 hours she was discharged, still nauseous.

Things did not get better from there. Tish and Ted were back at the ER and the clinic more than once, hoping against hope. She was given antibiotics, a steroid, and potassium. Then she developed a staph infection in her elbow, which swelled up like grapefruit; this required rehospitalization. Then she watched in horror as nurses, technicians, and cleaning crews in the hospital routinely ignored the quarantine

---

1. Nanovirus was prevalent that year and almost certainly the cause of her symptoms, making these drugs exactly the wrong treatment.

posted on her door—failing even to wash their hands in her room. She knew enough about medicine to know it was wrong, but she was at their mercy and was raised to be polite.

When Tish was finally discharged to a nursing home, her daughter Susan was given a quick overview of her mother's medications—now ballooned to 20 separate prescriptions—and sent on her way.

Tish was a college counselor and helped many young people find their way in life. Along with Ted, an architect, she raised three daughters and served on the boards of several museums and theaters in her Iowa town. At 80, she still had all of her faculties and had the help of her very intelligent, educated daughter. Despite these advantages, it would take her another week to unravel this dangerous bag of sometimes-conflicting medicines—one of which was not even her prescription—to get her sleeping pills administered at night instead of in the morning, to have her original symptoms treated, and to finally get home. Tish was lucky to get out of medical care alive.

When she told me this story, the question Tish asked was typical of her. Instead of being angry, she was worried about others who might be more frail. She asked, "What would happen to a patient in that situation with dementia? What if he couldn't ask questions?"

These are questions that keep me up at night. They should keep you up, too, because this is what you need to know: this happened in your hospital, your clinic, your convalescent care facility. Also, it happened in mine.

The other thing you need to know is that Tish is my mother-in-law and Susan is my wife. I dedicate this book to these two loving and important women in my life. I am hoping you will join me in making healthcare safe for them and your family, as well.

Contents

To download the appendix figures visit
ManagementontheMend.org. The passcode is journey.

Delivering
Better Healthcare,
an Introduction

Tish is not alone. Every day hundreds or thousands of people like her come to medical providers with illness and injury only to be mistreated and overcharged. Ninety-eight percent of the time this harm is not the fault of individual caregivers but of our healthcare system in general. Our processes for treating people are so fundamentally broken that mistakes are inevitable.

The debate over whether the nation has a sustainable healthcare system is over. Decades of rising costs and poor quality proved it does not.[2]

The question has been how to address the problems. This is no small query. Not only do we need to mend our disjointed processes for delivering care, we in healthcare need to respond to an array of changing laws, new payment proposals, and quality measures. Those who are not adaptive are about to get run over.

---

2. In just one example, the United States ranked last in quality out of 11 industrialized nations in a 2014 Commonwealth Fund study. We also were last in measures of efficiency, access to care, equity, and healthy lives. Accessed January 7, 2014. http://www.commonwealthfund.org/publications/press-releases/2014/jun/us-health-system-ranks-last

In response, some healthcare organizations have begun to learn and apply improvement techniques. Even the proudest physicians and medical institutions have had to admit flaws and launch coordinated efforts to remove waste and thereby improve quality and reduce cost in the system. That is the good news.

So many hospitals and health systems are using lean tools that *lean healthcare* has become a movement of sorts. Sometimes it is a punch line, unfortunately, because the bad news is that these programs have a fundamental flaw that threatens to derail even the most muscular efforts. In one hospital after another, I see the quest for positive change isolated as a discrete project, divorced from the daily work of managers, separate from the "real" business of the organization. People are stopping at reform when a revolution is required. The result is a vicious cycle of energetic hope followed by failure to create sustainable change.

In the six years since I left my position as CEO of a major cradle-to-grave health system in Wisconsin in order to help others achieve the kind of breakthrough transformations we built at ThedaCare Inc., I have spent most of my time in other people's hospitals and clinics. Every time I am invited to lecture or present findings to executive boards, I have one stipulation. Part of the visit must include a substantive visit to the units or offices where care is taking place.

After more than 145 such visits in 15 countries—and continuing at a rate of two or three new sites every month—I understand why I am seeing hope and failure in nearly equal measure. Teams of clinicians and administrators using lean thinking are making breakthroughs every week as they increase quality and reduce costs. But the essential transformation of the organization is not happening due to some basic misunderstandings about lean in healthcare.

The most common problem I see is that leaders fail to recognize the magnitude of change that will be required and that change extends to the leaders on a personal level. People set out on a lean journey thinking that improvement work will be the job of a few staff experts or consultants who will guide some projects. These projects will improve operations; people will learn how to initiate new improvements; and gradually, the theory goes, the organization will become lean. When I see this kind of attempt taking place, it always looks to me like the leaders have simply handed over the keys to the consultants or the improvement staff and expected them to return with something new, high performing, and sustainable in place of the old organization. This does not work.

Lean cannot be grafted onto an organization like the limb of a different tree. As anyone who has studied a little horticulture knows, a grafted limb will not transform the host tree into something new.

So, for the record, lean healthcare is not an improvement program. It is an operating system within a management system that requires a complete cultural transformation[3]. In a lean hospital, the job of every frontline caregiver is to practice medicine and to find and solve problems; every manager and executive is there to support the work of the frontline caregivers. Those are the two jobs available in a lean organization: problem solver and problem solver support staff. The CEO is support staff; his or her job is to identify and remove barriers so that problem solvers, such as inpatient hospitalist physicians and the newest x-ray technicians, can see and solve problems.

Most healthcare organizations could not look more different from the lean model. Management thinking is mostly descended from Alfred Sloan, the General Motors CEO and dominant force in twentieth-century

---

3. An illustration of a lean healthcare organization, where the management system provides structure for the operating system, is available in the appendix, figure 1.

business practices in the United States. Sloan's method—innovative at the time—relied on financial statistics to guide the business, emphasized clear chains of hierarchy, and focused on return on investment. Sloan philosophies created Management by Objectives. This common style of leadership creates a situation in which a CEO tells a senior leader, "Go out and start a lean initiative. Do whatever it takes. Go fast. We will judge you based on lean's success."

And that is the beginning of a lean healthcare failure.

I know how it happens. With the best intentions, I also did this as CEO. My former employer, ThedaCare, is a complete cradle-to-grave health system with five hospitals, dozens of clinics, home healthcare, mental healthcare, hospice, and innovative new programs all the time. It is the largest employer in northeast Wisconsin. In the early 2000s, we knew that a lean transformation would be a very big job, but I was enthusiastic and eager to be started on our lean transformation.

For the first three or four months, I led the lean effort by getting regular updates on our progress and encouraging the lean experts to think big. I told our lean consultant that he had my full support, and then I went back to my real job: fighting fires, developing strategic plans, and reviewing financial reports. That was the role of the CEO as I understood it.

Then our lean expert, or *sensei*,[4] told me to get out of my office and get involved. So, I did. I joined cross-functional teams—alongside physicians, nurses, patients, pharmacists, and complete outsiders—on rapid-improvement events. Sometimes, we were improving the flow of patient care in a Labor and Delivery unit. Or, we were mapping the route that patients took through our system and imagining a better way, with fewer hand-offs, less waiting time, and less waste.

---

4.   A Japanese term meaning an expert who teaches and mentors.

At the front line of care, working on teams, I saw that lean would utterly transform our culture if we did this right. Here was an improvement methodology that engaged our frontline people—the same ones who knew the problems intimately. I had a heady glimpse of an organization filled with problem solvers. But I still did not yet know what I did not know, including how I might need to change.

ThedaCare produced some breakthrough results in those early years, when we were running three to five rapid-improvement events per week throughout the organization. Teams used lean tools to cut in half the number of minutes it took for a cardiac patient to receive a life-saving angioplasty. In the spirit of continuous improvement, subsequent teams cut the time nearly in half again. Teamwork reduced time-to-treatment for stroke victims. Another team nearly eliminated incidence of babies born too early due to induced labor.

Cutting waste out of processes produced real savings. At one time, we were saving an average of $45,000 for every rapid-improvement event we did, week in and week out.

Even then, however, we were setting ourselves up for failure. Our leaders should have been learning strategy deployment, visual management, and how to support the model cell.[5] We should have been redesigning the tasks and patterns of our work lives. Instead, we were using old leadership methods and expecting new results.

Right around year three of our lean journey, we began realizing that we were hitting walls. Quality was uneven and stubbornly unimproved in some areas. Some projects that were celebrated as breakthroughs could not be sustained. Employee satisfaction was down, and people kept

---

5. A model cell is an area where lean thinking and organizational resources have been intensely focused to create transformation that is mission-critical. The model cell is used as a demonstration and teaching tool for the rest of the organization, to learn about the coming changes.

falling back into old patterns. Unit managers complained of getting squeezed while trying to manage two ways at once. Meanwhile, after three years and hundreds of rapid-improvement events, many of our people still did not even know the meaning of *lean*.

Now, I know from visiting dozens of hospitals and clinics struggling with the exact same issues that these are the symptoms of management by objectives in a lean environment, which simply does not work.[6] Lean demands real, system-wide change by every manager, starting at the top. Senior leaders cannot delegate a profound cultural shift; they cannot expect others to embrace change while they continue working in the same old command-and-control style, checking the numbers without really understanding how the numbers were or were not achieved.

These are the biggest problems I see as I visit healthcare organizations: failure of leadership to engage in the substance of change and mistaking the lean operating and management system for a quick improvement program. In many ways, these are two faces of the same problem. Fortunately, I have also seen enough organizations launch productive, energetic lean initiatives—or correct the course of a stalled effort—that I am confident there is a right way to go about this.

For many years, I have been reluctant to prescribe a single best way to launch and conduct a lean effort. I was a student alongside so many others, discovering the role of lean in healthcare. At this point, however, an awful lot of data have accumulated. Over the past decade, hundreds of healthcare organizations around the world have been experimenting with lean, and I have been privileged to get an insider's view of the arc of many of those journeys.

---

6.   In a lean environment, we follow more closely the ideals of "management by process," described by W. Edwards Deming in his 1982 book *Out of the Crisis*.

Now I am ready to say that there is a right way to embark on a lean journey. We—by which I mean me and leaders from dozens of health systems committed to lean transformations—have discovered a model for a lean transformation that works, and this book describes it through the people who are doing the work. It is a story of many journeys joined together and told through the best practices and fresh ideas found in hospitals and clinics across North America. The organizations in these pages have not all followed precisely the steps I will lay out in this book, but what others and I have learned from their journeys has helped inform this path.

For instance, we can travel to California's Bay Area, where the Palo Alto Medical Foundation has 27 clinics and 1,000 physicians in 38 specialties serving 780,000 patients. When I met senior leaders there in 2011, they had a name brand, great practitioners, and good patient satisfaction scores. But leaders were worried. A very well-regarded HMO was moving aggressively into their Silicon Valley territory, and leaders were pretty sure that they were not financially competitive. There was a lot of waste in the system, and those 27 sites—the result of a recent merger of three companies under a new corporation—often had 27 wildly different personalities. Leaders knew they needed unity and better processes to meet the threat.

By this time, a few organizations had discovered the power of beginning a lean transformation with a model cell. So, Palo Alto Medical Foundation's senior leaders focused their energy on a large multispecialty clinic in the industrialized suburb of Fremont.[7] To make the project manageable, they opted to first transform half of the operation, comprising the 50-physician primary care clinic.

---

7. Palo Alto leadership did a good bit of planning and prework before launching into a model cell, of course. We will explore the necessary foundational work in chapter 2.

Cross-functional teams, including doctors, assistants, nurses, patients, and administrative staff, began redesigning the workflow and offices in late 2011. Specifically, they wanted to know whether they could simultaneously improve service to their patients—measured by better outcomes—cut waiting time, and create better work flow in order to take some of the pressure off of their often overworked staff.

Working with the doctors, the teams took some radical actions. They removed all individual physician offices in favor of a central seating area for medical staff where every doctor sits beside or across from a medical assistant in order to aid the flow of communication.

Every morning there is a quick huddle with the core team of physicians and assistants to talk about the day ahead, review staffing issues, and highlight problematic cases. Using this time to collectively anticipate problems has reduced the amount of firefighting the staff must do during the day.

Incoming telephone call traffic was also completely reimagined and designed, eventually enabling clinic staff to resolve 50% of new questions or requests on first contact, as opposed to the previous rate of near-zero resolution on first contact. New systems also dramatically improved patients' access to same-day appointments.

Newly designed processes helped physicians complete all note taking and close patient files while still in the exam room with the patient. Physicians agreed that their documentation was better in this new process, since they did not have to remember the details of many appointments over a busy day.

Within a few months, doctors were going home on time, their work completed. The daily accumulation of tasks in their in-baskets was cut in half. All this was accomplished without hiring new employees and while the clinic was steadily gaining new patients.

Once physicians were happy with the changes and could brag to colleagues about getting out of the office at a decent hour, spreading model-cell design to all the clinics was a lot easier. By mid-2012—less than a year after the redesign began—leaders were spreading out to the 25 other Palo Alto Medical Foundation clinics. In 18 months, the core components of the model cell were up and running in every clinic in the system.[8]

In February 2014, *Consumer Reports* rated Palo Alto Medical Foundation as the best medical group in the crowded San Francisco/Bay Area.[9]

"Lean has been a tipping point toward cultural integration for us," says Michael Conroy, MD, chief medical officer for the organization and a leader of the transformation efforts. "We always had a culture focused on service. Now, we all know how to make improvements, too. Physicians, assistants, nurses—they know how to identify a problem and create an action plan. We are speaking a common language."

This is the reason that building a model cell is the first order of business on the lean journey: with a life-sized, three-dimensional working model that people can gather around, touch, talk about, and work through, employees develop a common understanding of lean and continuous-improvement practices.

Now let's say your first model cell is working great and your employees are gathered around gazing in wonder and one physician who is new to the ideas turns to another and asks, "Why are we doing this?"

At this moment, you need people who can answer that question with a core message. To do that, you need clearly stated values and principles,

---

8. The best practices discovered while spreading the model-cell work to every clinic in the system will be discussed in chapter 6.

9. 2014 was the first year that *Consumer Reports* rated and ranked medical groups in California.

and so the next step in a transformation is developing and teaching these core ideas and guidelines.

Values are the highest beliefs and aspirations of the leaders; these are what steer the company. They might include putting the customers first, finding joy in work, or continuous learning. Principles guide behavior, which should always lead toward satisfying the organization's values. The scientific method should be a principle common to all lean transformations, as this is what guides improvements and decisions.

If physician 2 in the example above replies, "It's for a new focus on quality; we're using the scientific method to find and correct errors in care delivery," you are one giant step closer to getting everyone on board. Clearly stating the organization's values and principles should reassure employees who fear change.[10] Adhering to those values is part of the pact that needs to be formed between senior leaders and staff; it is the promise that change will be to everyone's benefit.

For instance, when Paul O'Neill took over as CEO of Alcoa, the world's largest aluminum producer, in 1987, he told a room full of anxious Wall Street investors that the top concern for his administration would be worker safety—not shareholder value or return on investment. The safety of all workers would drive Alcoa, he said.

At Alcoa sites around the world, O'Neill told employees they were part of an effort to achieve perfect worker safety through process improvement. Whether employees were processing expense sheets or raw bauxite, the goal was zero workplace injuries, he told everyone. O'Neill, who later became secretary of the U.S. Treasury, backed up his belief with a relentless focus on improving conditions and turned

---

10. Some employees will fear the word "lean," which got a bad reputation in some quarters due to failed efforts by companies looking for a quick fix. Some organizations opt not to use the term "lean." I will continue to do so, however, because lean thinking, which arose out of the Toyota Production System, is exactly what I am talking about.

Alcoa around, financially and culturally. To investment analysts this was amazing. Without seeming to focus on shareholder value, he achieved it to a remarkable degree.

We will dive more deeply into best practices surrounding the adoption and teaching of values and principles further on, but for now, remember that values should strike at the heart of our humanity. "Becoming lean" is not a value.

Next, build the infrastructure for your effort with a team of lean facilitators. Some organizations call this group internal consultants or a lean promotion office. Whatever they are called, these people are the human engine for your effort. Like step two—stating the values and principles—this step will naturally occur in conjunction with the model-cell planning phase.

There are many good examples of well-planned lean improvement teams, and they tend to have a few things in common. Robust teams comprise about 1% of the FTE[11] workforce and offer two-year rotations on the team as a clear path for advancement, and the team leader reports directly to the CEO. This is not a back office in which to park a few earnest but ineffective improvers. If it is, nobody will take the effort seriously. I know from long experience that energy and magnetism are required to move people out of their comfortable ruts.

The next step is perhaps the most challenging: redesign your management system to support the lean transformation. This is the step that most companies either ignored or never really understood during the initial decade of the lean movement in North American healthcare. Senior leaders acted as though lean was a transformation for the improvement

---

11. Full-time equivalent. At ThedaCare, we had 5,500 employees on the payroll, and many of those people were working part-time, adding up to 3,700 FTEs. So, the ThedaCare Improvement System office usually had about 36 team members during my tenure.

staff and the front line only. This often left managers at all levels trying to serve the needs of two systems: old-fashioned and lean.

A real transformation means bringing everyone along and making sure all efforts are aligned with the business' strategies. At ThedaCare, Kim Barnas, who was a vice president and then president of the hospitals division, led the effort to redesign the work content and schedule of every supervisor, manager, and executive, introducing standard work,[12] known goals, and clear accountability for every leader. Then, she taught other healthcare organizations to do the same, replicating the system across North America.[13]

Do you remember that great model cell? By this point, with your management system redesign in place and the model cell up and running, word has spread about the new ideas, the leap-ahead in improvement. The manager and director of that area are stars, and there is mounting pressure from other parts of the organization for a model cell of their own. Only now—after the model is running smoothly, values have been stated and spread, the central improvement team is up and running, and your management system is redesigned—should you actually spread the work of that model cell.

Let the demand for this exciting new system build. Encourage advocates to tell their colleagues and direct reports about the model cell; feed stories about progress of this work into any available communications channels. The model cell that has been designed for everyone's benefit should help sell itself.

---

12. Standard work is a written set of step-by-step instructions for completing a task using the best-known methods. Standard work is written and agreed upon by a team and should be changed only by a team that has found a better method.

13. Kim Barnas's book describing this work is *Beyond Heroes: A Lean Management System for Healthcare* (ThedaCare Center for Healthcare Value: 2014).

If you doubt that, think about Dr. Conroy in Palo Alto. In just 18 months, 450 physicians in his organization agreed to give up their personal offices. They were not bribed or strong-armed. Those doctors looked at a better system, saw that their colleagues were going home on time with the day's work finished, and decided they wanted those benefits as well.

This does not mean that spreading the work of the model cell throughout an organization is without challenges. I have seen organizations face many unforeseen hurdles to spreading the work over the years and, luckily, some of those leaders have come up with valuable ideas to share in the chapters ahead.

And now we cross a threshold. To this point, most of the work of a lean journey has been focused at gemba,[14] creating frontline teams of problem solvers, embedding the scientific method into the culture and practices, and creating new ways to work. It will quickly become apparent, however, that your shiny new model cells are living in hostile management environments, where long-established policies and habits suited to management by objectives seek to destroy or undermine your good work. So, the threshold we cross in this book's section II is into the boardrooms and executive suites where system-wide changes need to be addressed in support services, especially in human resources, finance, and information technology.

After personally witnessing a few epic battles between lean change agents and the good people of human resources, I recommend that you forge an early partnership with HR. You will need their help with new training regimes, succession planning, hiring criteria, and all kinds of organizational development activities. I will go into depth on the changes that

---

14. A Japanese word often used by Toyota Production System practitioners, "gemba" means the place where real value is created. In a hospital, gemba is located wherever caregivers are directly helping patients.

need to be made in the chapter on HR in the new world, but for now, let me just say: prepare for a closer working relationship. Remember that every change made in clinical or administrative processes will reverberate through the organization, sometimes in surprising ways.

For Rachelle Schultz, CEO of Winona Health Services, the surprise was how the annual budget started sticking out like a sore thumb. Her organization began its lean initiative in 2008, and by the third year, teams had made great improvements by producing and using real-time data to learn the truth about work flows and processes and to find improvement opportunities.

The entire organization was getting accustomed to seeing now (the current condition) instead of then (the past, sometimes the distant past). For a few weeks every year, however, they would set aside their current information systems in order to produce a budget—the future seen through the lens of the past—that was wrong from the moment it was published.

"Since we could never accurately predict everything, we were spending more time explaining the budget variances than we were calibrating the business and figuring out how to get to where we wanted to go," Rachelle says.

"Meanwhile, we were forecasting the near-term future from up-to-date data, and that proved to be far more accurate and agile. Having a budget too was like keeping electronic medical records and a paper patient file, as well. It didn't make sense to do both."

Rachelle worked with her board of trustees, executives, and department managers on needs and expectations. She and her team investigated what forecasting software could and could not do. Within a little more than a year, they had retired the annual distraction of creating a budget. At the same time, they are able to produce forecasts based on current conditions for six or eight quarters into the future, thus helping leaders make decisions now.

This is one of the hallmarks of a lean transformation: support services—HR, finance, IT—shift focus from producing their own inward-looking reports to actively supporting the organization's improvement efforts. Instead of producing budgets, Rachelle's finance team started providing unit managers with personalized accounting services to help them understand business reporting.

At Salem Health in Oregon's Willamette Valley, a lean transformation meant that information technology experts could begin focusing on projects that directly benefit patients, such as reducing hospital-acquired infections.

Salem Health is a not-for-profit system of hospitals, clinics, and outpatient services. It is the largest private employer in Oregon's capital city and has the busiest emergency department in the state. Like a few other healthcare organizations, it had put considerable energy into integrating operations data with analytics[15] to create something we refer to as clinical business intelligence.[16] In 2013, while studying operations data, the clinical business intelligence team saw a real opportunity to improve patient care. The rate of hospital-acquired *Clostridium difficile* infections, commonly referred to as *C. diff*, was stubbornly high. Using previously collected and new data, a team of physicians, administrators, and lean experts targeted a medical unit and a surgical unit that, together, had been responsible for 99 *C. diff* cases in 2012.

---

15. Analytics is the search for, and study of, meaningful patterns in data.

16. "Hospitals Are Finally Starting to Put Real Time Data to Use," *Harvard Business Review*. Last accessed January 8, 2015. https://hbr.org/2014/11/hospitals-are-finally-starting-to-put-real-time-data-to-use

The new annual goal, the team decided, was zero. Using the problem-solving cycle plan-do-study-act (PDSA) and analytics, the team developed a four-pronged approach to tracking, treatment, and prevention. In the two months after the team's plans were fully implemented, the two units reported a total of one *C. diff* case. Next, the team moved on to using clinical business intelligence to identify the infection cases that originated in the community versus the hospital in order to track the problem to its sources and attack it there.

This is why everyone in a healthcare organization goes to work everyday: to save lives, to restore health, to avoid harm. Work in support departments—to create budgets, collate data about the past, and process internal forms—is not anyone's end goal or life's work. People in support services want to be more involved in the work of healing people and improving systems. And frontline caregivers need their help.

Over the past decade in hundreds of healthcare organizations, this is the path we have discovered for transformation: lay the foundation, build a model cell, establish the values and principles that will guide the work, create a central improvement office, redesign the frontline management system, and spread the work throughout the system. Then realign the organization's policies and practices, especially in human resources, finance, and information technology, to support this work. There will be barriers and curveballs, such as new payment schemes and a medical education system that keeps churning out heroes instead of team players, but we will work through those, too.

This path goes beyond the action plan that I laid out in my 2010 book, *On the Mend*,[17] to focus more clearly on management and the entire organization. I have learned much in the past five years. I have been privileged to meet with hundreds of healthcare leaders anxious to change

---

17. John Toussaint, MD, and Roger A. Gerard, PhD, *On the Mend: Revolutionizing Healthcare to Save Lives and Transform the Industry* (Lean Enterprise Institute: 2010)

and then follow their journeys through the successes and setbacks. I have expanded my focus and emphasized the managerial and organizational elements of successful transformation journeys because I have learned how fragmented healthcare organizations are. The individual units sub-specialties and clinics are usually like marbles in a box; they bang into one another without ever working together for the good of the patient. This is true everywhere. As new methods and technologies have emerged, hospitals have simply added them in on the fly without reconsidering upstream and downstream processes. The resulting disorganization does not best serve the patients.

Individual hospitals and organizations across the country have certainly made great strides in helping many people some of the time. But the achievements are isolated to certain areas or therapies. Leaders rarely consider changing the interconnected *system*. Just as a patient's health is not limited to a heart or kidney alone, it is true that healthcare improve-ment is not just about new cancer therapies or central-line infection reduction projects. Lean healthcare is about creating a biologic organism in balance. Let's get started.

Part I

A Revolution
in Six Steps

1

Laying
the Foundation

Before every improvement project begins, there is essential prework. This is when leaders collect baseline data, select team members, and identify the project scope. Failure to attend to prework can set people galloping off in opposite directions, so it is critical to the success of a project even if it is not very glamorous.

Prework for an organization's first model cell will be far more personal and emotional for senior leaders than it is for others. The first step in your prework, after all, is recognizing that change is necessary. Step two is admitting that you need to change. Not just your organization. *You.* You might need to change only a little. Most of us need to change a lot.

If you pride yourself on your ability to make quick decisions and set people straight, your leadership style is going to need an overhaul. If you have decided that you can delegate the work of change to middle management, you need to adjust that, too.

Most of us get to leadership positions on the strength of deep knowledge in our field and a talent for swaying opinions. Along the way, most of us learn to love being the one with the answers, the vision, the plan. And there is nothing so heady as gathering together a group of smart, capable people and saying, "This is what I've decided to do."

Lean organizations, on the other hand, need leaders who respect the knowledge and experience of the people on the front line of care. Instead of assuming that you have—or should have—the answer, it is your job as a leader to ask questions and help others use the right tools and processes to solve the problems they see. The lean leader's role is first as a student, learning how work is actually being accomplished, and then finding what he or she can do to help facilitate improvement. Only when people know how processes are performed can those processes be improved. Only when people learn to see with new eyes and to use lean tools can they begin to help others improve.

You can take down organizational barriers to solving problems, but you cannot solve everyone's problems. Learning this offers tremendous freedom. It is an adjustment that I have seen many executives embrace over the years, and most report becoming better connected to their organizations for it.

Still, some healthcare leaders will try to avoid this personal transformation and delegate the effort instead. This never works. If you delegate the lean transformation to someone else and the effort fails, a little more distrust and cynicism will creep into your organization. If you delegate lean to someone else and it succeeds, your organization will be improving without you. If you continue to lead the old way—dictating from above—while your people learn to solve problems, you will be creating a chaos of expectations. People will constantly wonder whether they should be awaiting orders from above or finding and fixing problems at the front line.

To be fair, it is possible to get some good results even when leadership is disconnected from the effort. An improvement team can convene in just about any hospital and score huge savings right away. But when the leadership is disconnected from the effort, a team can save $500,000 in the first week and the organization will gain nothing.

Does that last statement sound absurd? You saved a half-million dollars. How is that nothing? Having been through this exercise hundreds of times, I can tell you exactly how you will fail to get the benefit of that $500,000. Your HR director will tell you that he is not equipped to redeploy the three full-time-equivalent nurses and two technicians that were deemed unnecessary in the new work flow. So the CFO cannot remove those FTEs from expenses in the budget.[18] Or, let's say the team has overhauled the process of caring for the frail elderly, ensuring better home healthcare and posthospitalization follow-ups. Those interventions were right for the patients and kept them out of crisis but did not pay nearly as much as hospitalizations.[19] The CFO in these cases will likely pronounce lean a disaster for the bottom line.

Senior executives, caught within their own work silos and accustomed to maximizing the financial performance of their departments, have been rewarded throughout their careers for thinking first about their own budgets. Like the CEO and everyone else, they must learn to put the patient first. Until the day that senior executives are on board and working together for the patient, every improvement made can be whittled away to nothing.

---

18. This conversation will change dramatically when executives know that redeploying people is not the responsibility of HR alone. Senior leaders will together develop standard work to create a system that matches people made redundant with new jobs.

19. This was ThedaCare's experience, recounted in my article "Essential Elements for the Success of the ACO Model," *Journal of the American Medical Association*, 2013; 310(13):1341–1342.

And this is where the next, painful bit of prework comes in and it might involve group therapy. If your senior executive team is dysfunctional—if people cannot agree on the facts, if they are distrustful and dismissive of one another—you will need to work on that first. Breaking down individual silos is hard enough. Doing that in an environment of disrespect is nearly impossible.

At ThedaCare, our senior executive team had plenty of squabbles and blind spots. At the insistence of leaders from HR and organizational development, we started meeting for two-day sessions every quarter that were intended to help us improve our relationships with one another. We worked on becoming better listeners and tried to stop jumping to conclusions. These were sometimes excruciating sessions—particularly when my colleagues were invited to discuss the deficits in my leadership style. A friend of mine in another healthcare organization hired a marriage and family therapist to sit in on his senior executive meetings until everyone learned to listen to one another.

In the time since then, I have become convinced that there is a shortcut to team unity: focus on creating common goals. In many organizations, senior leaders are judged by key performance indicators that pit them against each other. These must be eliminated before the leadership group can set about finding the handful of organizational goals to guide all of your decision making: your True North.[20] Focusing on finding those shared goals is far more productive than interpersonal group therapy. When there is no stated agreement on what is most important for the organization, fierce opinions and hard feelings can rule the discussion.

---

20. True North is the handful of metrics used to guide decisions and gauge progress. True North metrics are stable and few. For instance, one of ThedaCare's True North metrics year over year is preventable mortality. The goal is zero. Every year, senior leaders set new targets against the metric to push us closer to the goal.

Finding True North begins, for most teams, with going to see what *good* looks like. Find the organizations with the best track records in quality and cost of care and those that have a robust model cell, and ask the leaders how they got there. Ask about their True North. In lean healthcare, there is a tradition of sharing goals and results with others, so the best organizations are accustomed to giving tours and answering questions.

The most successful executive teams I have worked with have all toured at least one lean hospital or health system and then agreed on a process to figure out what good will look like for them. This is necessary for envisioning the future state, and it must be a team activity in order to build senior-management trust and agreement. This requires being in a room together and taking a hard look at reality, including your current safety, quality, and cost records. If your organization were really high performing, how would those numbers change? What would your hospital-acquired infection rate be? How about your rate of 30-day rehospitalizations?

Hire a coach or facilitator with deep lean knowledge to come in and guide this discussion. Overall, I would say that 95% of the executive teams I have worked with have used an outside coach to help these early discussions.[21] The outcome should be your organizational performance goals in five areas: safety, quality, people, delivery, and cost. For most health systems, metrics in these five areas will be your True North. The difficulty of this task lies in choosing a mere handful of metrics—more like five than 15—and establishing the goals for those metrics.

As leaders clearly identify the organization's current reality and its goals, they will also be defining the gap. And in that gap, you may find a useful tool for your lean transformation. What you are looking for is a lever.

---

21. A coach is a content expert—often a consultant—who is trusted to provide feedback on personal and team performance. A sensei has deeper knowledge in lean tools and principles and vast experience working in a lean environment. A sensei is often a coach, but not every coach is a sensei.

All organizations suffer from a little stasis, some resistance to change. So, a lever is needed to get people moving forward. Leaders of Virginia Mason Medical Center in Seattle famously used the 2004 medical-error death of a 69-year-old woman who was injected with an antiseptic fluid instead of dye prior to surgery to push urgently for systemic change. Johns Hopkins Children's Center leaders became open about their need for improvement following the death of an 18-month-old girl of dehydration. A little openness about the harm that is already caused, illustrated in a single case, can be a powerful call to action.

Be careful, however, about using too broad a brush. When ThedaCare was planning for lean in 2002, I became fond of pointing out just how many medical errors we made on a regular basis. This was overwhelming and dispiriting instead of the call for action that I intended. A single case, however, used to illustrate the larger issues can be an emotional rallying cry.

The final two activities are not necessarily part of building the model cell's foundation; both can be concurrent with the model cell's launch. It is good, however, for leaders to begin planning for the impact that these big changes will have on people and think about ways to manage the change.

Communicate the coming changes, especially to managers who will need to explain it to their direct reports. If I had this moment to do over, I would keep the message simple. I would tell everyone that we are going to change the way we do things in order to deliver the safest patient care in America and that we will be solving problems using the methodology of the ThedaCare Improvement System, and I would have offered managers resources for further information so they could begin to become familiar with the concepts.

Finally, think about the big voices in your organization—everyone has them—and prepare to begin a dialogue about the benefits of creating a model cell to test the benefits of lean. Maybe your cardiologists or ob-gyns are smart, vocal, and well liked. Maybe one group or another is openly disgruntled. Prepare to use this to your advantage by getting those physicians engaged. Explain that the entire focus of the model cell is improving quality for patients and, with their help, the organization will become radically different. Solicit ideas and get these big voices on improvement teams.

Some of the most disgruntled physicians have made the best change agents, in my experience. When they have helped launch the model cell, these are the men and women who will sell it to the rest of the organization. Let's start building.

2

The Model
Cell

That room was a mess. Everywhere I looked, there were cardboard boxes saggy with overuse, all of them repurposed so many times it was hard to tell which bit of scrawled writing was relevant. Plastic boxes stood in for drug delivery carts, and in the aisles between the refuse, nurses walked like trapeze artists, focused and quietly counting their steps.

What I really remember though is the light in their eyes, their excitement as these nurses introduced me to our inpatient unit of the future. Here, they pointed out, was a central open area for physicians and nurses to meet. All patient doors opened into this central square so that nobody would be stuck at the far end of a dark hallway.

Patient rooms were all private and fitted with special room-darkening shades to allow every test and many procedures to be done in the patient's room instead of wheeling her all around the hospital. X-rays, endoscopy, ultrasounds, radiologic procedures—everything except an MRI would be done in the room. Here was the two-sided cabinet with sliding shelves that allowed nurses to restock patient rooms without disturbing the patient. Here was the standardized placement of every necessity on those shelves, from washcloths to drugs.

Over the weeks of work on this, our first model cell, this team and others had worked together to completely redesign and standardize the patient experience in our hospitals. They cut down on the steps nurses had to take, the amount of time they spent running around looking for things, and the time patients had to spend waiting on an inefficient system. As a result, once the cell started serving patients, our quality performance shot up across a dozen measures; patients would report that they were "very satisfied" with their care 90% of the time instead of 68%; and the cost of caring for a patient on the new unit would drop by 30%. This model cell, dubbed Collaborative Care, became the standard for inpatient care at all ThedaCare hospitals.

Everyone remembers that first model cell. When done right, it is a revolution instead of the usual evolutionary change in work processes. It is the critical first step in a lean journey because the model cell becomes your organization's introduction to lean thinking. With this cell, you tell everyone, "This is how lean thinking looks here, in our particular circumstances."

Creating this cell is exciting and also upsetting because there is the danger that your revolution can go terribly awry. To help you keep the wheels on the track, I have identified five guidelines to follow that will also help to define the model-cell concept.

1. The model cell must be focused on a business problem that is important to the organization. The team should be able to clearly state the business case for this work. For instance, in the example above, our business case was: "The inpatient experience is disjointed and confusing. The quality results are

not reliable, leading to poor customer satisfaction and patient harm."[22] When there is agreement on the business case, the team is better focused.

Relevancy is just as important as clarity here. If everyone knows that your biggest challenge is too much patient demand on a small, aging facility, the model cell must address that issue in some way. This could mean that the model cell is focused on redesigning the work of a congested emergency department or designing a new ambulatory surgery center. If hospital leaders choose for the model cell to chip away at a problem on the outskirts of an organization's needs, such as projects focused on resupplying pharmacy cabinets, it will signal leadership's lack of commitment to change.

2. The model cell runs an inch wide and a mile deep. This means that the scope of the project must be limited, usually to one unit or clinic, even though the ideas being tested are intended for the entire organization. And knowledge of lean thinking, problem-solving practices, the management system, and tools must be sunk deep into the people within the project scope. Every successful transformation I have seen includes some kind of intensive lean training—done on the gemba by doing the work, not in the classroom—for everyone connected with the model cell.

3. Create a new system based on standard work. The team will not be making tweaks or small adjustments to current processes. It will instead create new work processes and will use the scientific method to address any problems that arise. This means that the

---

22. Causing harm to one's customers is, after all, a bad and unsustainable business model.

model-cell team must be trained to write standard work that is clear, useful, and accepted by the people who will use it.

4. Tie the model-cell work to True North. If your safety goals are to eliminate patient falls, for instance, this should be reflected in the scope of work for the model cell. Everyone should get accustomed to coordinating improvement work with the organization's handful of key metrics.

5. This work must involve senior leadership if at all possible. If the CEO and COO are not joining the team on at least one of the model cell's project weeks, or if the work is not championed by a member of the executive leadership, you need to stop and reassess. This is difficult work that requires real change from the organization and your people. The hand on the helm must be willing to change, as well.

In the big picture, you will find that the model cell has two distinct and almost contradictory roles. It is a testing center where people can experiment with ideas, embrace failure as a path for learning, and put new concepts into action. It will also be the demonstration exhibit—the results of your finest efforts that you will then use to sell lean healthcare ideas and spread these new methods to the rest of your organization.

The model cell will also be the front line of debates between early adopters of change and the skeptics. At every organization I have visited, there have been stories about battles large and small between physicians who embrace lean and those who thought the old ways were good enough. People in the model cell need to be prepared for close—even hostile—questioning.

To get a better picture of a model cell in action, let's go to the Lehigh Valley Health Network. A system with four hospitals, dozens of clinics, and 14,000 employees that serves urban Allentown, Pennsylvania, and the bucolic suburbs of Pennsylvania Dutch country, Lehigh's patient population was growing fast in 2011. A lot faster than they had anticipated.

At the Muhlenberg facility in the town of Bethlehem, new studies predicted that the annual volume of 54,000 patients would soon rise to 70,000. One solution was 25 new beds in the ED, which would require an addition to the building with a new roofline, according to an architectural consultant. Total cost would be $25 million. Lehigh Valley senior executives told the ED leadership that, in view of the current healthcare economics, they could allocate just $5 million over the next year or two. The ED could expand into its current waiting room and an adjacent underutilized hospital lobby, but otherwise the ED was landlocked.

Meanwhile, the 30 chairs in the emergency waiting room were often full with patients waiting too long. "The ED would barely get cleared out by 7 a.m. when the daytime rush would start all over again. We knew we weren't meeting customer requirements," says Lean Director Dale Lucht, an engineer who had moved to healthcare from manufacturing.

Leaders knew that the old model—growth equals more beds and more square footage—would not work. They needed a new way to think about the physical requirements of patient care.

Using reports from their patient-satisfaction survey service, Press Ganey, plus informal surveys of patients in the ED, the team saw that patient satisfaction showed a steady decline as length of stay increased. The team decided to focus on two key patient-satisfaction drivers: the time it took from patient arrival in the ED to see a provider and the time it took from patient arrival to actual treatment.

The business problem was clear. They had to reduce wait times, waiting-room congestion, and treatment delays while improving patient satisfaction to maintain or gain market share and while using less space.

Dr. Richard MacKenzie, a member of the original team that chose lean as their improvement model, recalls that they spotted their improvement opportunity in the "dwell time" of a certain population of the ED.

"At Muhlenberg, 75% of patients were discharged from the ED instead of being admitted to the hospital. Of those people, 20%–30% needed only one test or intervention. So, we reasoned that we could have a larger impact by reducing the dwell time for those patients," Dr. MacKenzie says. "Also, we could free up the space used by these patients if we could move them through the system faster."

Dr. MacKenzie asked Dale Lucht for help; Dale assigned Chris Kita, a lean coach also originally from manufacturing, and they put together a cross-functional team of clinical and nonclinical people and started working through ideas. As a team, they engaged a consultant, visited emergency departments that had been remodeled for efficiency, and debated the ideas they saw.

Out of these experiences, a conceptual model emerged with standardized roles and tasks. Before launching into an expensive remodel, the team first tested the concept with a rapid-cycle test.[23] They put incoming patients directly into treatment beds for evaluation—no waiting for triage in chairs—and then moved them to another area for treatment. At 5 p.m. on the day of the rapid-cycle test, the normally full waiting room was empty. A fractured arm was treated in 45 minutes. An appendicitis patient was evaluated and in the operating room within two hours of arrival.

The concept seemed solid, but the live test also uncovered many issues. So, with senior leadership now in full support, the team began their work in earnest.

---

23. This is a time-limited testing of ideas to see how they play out in reality. At Lehigh Valley, some rapid-cycle tests were called 12-hour model cells.

The team expanded to work on architectural designs. They relied heavily on the triage experience of frontline nurses to reimagine patient flow and care. Team members agreed on a new layout of the ED, with a 12-bed rapid-assessment unit—the patient's first stop—and then a 24-chair results waiting area. They used an enlarged engineering drawing of the proposed layout to create a tabletop model of their new ED and began simulating process and flow.

Patient charts from the rapid-cycle test day in the ED were used to represent actual patients (de-identified, of course) as they presented that day, in the same order and at the same time. Paper cutouts were even created to represent patients to visually humanize the simulation. "It was like a board game," Kita says, "but with real patient data and scenarios driving the play."

To test the feasibility of findings from the tabletop simulations, the team conducted many rapid-cycle tests and discovered the power of these tests to turn "what-if" statements proposed by skeptics into "what-did" happen reports, says Dr. MacKenzie. For example, for a few rapid-cycle tests, they used four treatment rooms to represent rapid-assessment exam rooms, and a nursing conference room with eight chairs was the results waiting area. For the what-if objections of ED physicians, Dr. MacKenzie could now walk through a simulation with his colleagues and play out how it would work.

Here, it is easy to see how important it is to have a doctor on board. "Without a credible physician champion, I'm not sure how you would pull this off," Kita says.

Dr. MacKenzie agrees that convincing his physician colleagues to try a new routine was a challenge. "Doctors tend toward perfectionism. They don't want to rush into the unknown. So we would put ideas to work for a limited time period—maybe for a six-hour rapid-cycle test. Then we could all look at the errors and the benefits," Dr. MacKenzie says.

"I remember one day of rapid-cycle testing when a fellow doctor confronted me at the beginning and said that none of the ideas were going to work. I said, 'Good. At the end of the day I want to hear about every single thing that's bad and doesn't work. Lean is about surfacing the errors. Every problem is an opportunity to improve upon the ideas.'

"At the end of the day, he conceded that the test went OK and offered some concrete suggestions for improvement," Dr. MacKenzie says.

There were plenty of experiments that went awry, of course. One day, they tried stationing one physician in the rapid-assessment unit and one physician assistant in the results waiting area. It was a kind of zone-defense play to see whether having one provider dedicated to treatments would speed waiting time in the chairs.

"It was horrible," Dr. MacKenzie says. "Length of stay went up by 40 minutes and we had to sign some patients out to the acute-care area to get testing."

As the new process jelled, the team found that their guiding principles should also be some of their key performance indicators:

1. Door-to-provider time should be less than 20 minutes.

2. Keep vertical patients vertical.[24]

3. Patients should spend less than one hour in the rapid-assessment unit.

4. Practice situational decision making.

---

24. Meaning, do not put ambulatory patients in a bed to await a diagnosis or test results.

The basic premise of the new process was fairly straightforward. Efficiency gains were made by doing standard work in parallel rather than sequentially. Patients walked into the ED and were immediately led back to a rapid-assessment room for evaluation and diagnosis. In the room, the patient met with an assessment team consisting of a registration clerk, a nurse, and a provider (either a physician or a qualified physician assistant).

The registration clerk had first priority with the patient and asked for necessary admitting information such as name, age, and insurance. The nurse was second and determined why the patient came to the ED while also gathering vital signs and history regarding medication, allergies, and other conditions. They found that this was usually the best unfiltered story of the patient's concerns, so the provider, who was already listening to everything the patient reported thus far, had to ask only a few additional questions to get to an impression and plan of care.

With the possible diagnoses determined, the provider can either write a script and discharge the patient directly from the assessment room or order additional treatment such as a splint or an x-ray and move the patient from the assessment room and into a chair in the results waiting area. For the patient, this is not aimless waiting to begin the healthcare process. This is waiting to begin the treatment that had already been determined.

If the provider determined that a patient required a comprehensive workup, the patient would be sent to the acute-care section of the ED. Patients arriving by ambulance were brought directly to the acute-care section and never saw the rapid-assessment unit.

The new process definitely moved people through the ED faster, but it also turned traditional priorities upside down, for both physicians and nurses. Because patients now spent less than one hour in the assessment room, beds were being turned over almost twice as fast as before.

And because the new layout put the provider workstations in close physical and visual proximity to the assessment rooms, providers were visually prompted to work at the rate of patient demand. This perturbed many providers and nurses. But as concerns were discussed and addressed through tabletop simulations and rapid-cycle tests, they slowly came to acceptance. At least, everyone agreed to give it a try.

Creating standard work for each role was key to creating consistency. Nursing roles were no longer longitudinal, with a nurse responsible for five or six patients for their entire stay, for instance. Instead, the roles became functional. The assessment nurse was solely responsible for getting patients assessed, not starting treatments or medications. The treatment nurse's responsibilities were to be alert to new orders in the patient's EMR[25] and to provide medications and treatment.

"This was completely different than our previous nursing model," notes Melissa Teitsworth, ED RN. "At first we thought there is absolutely no way this is going to work. It was tough for us to stick only to our role to make the process work. We are used to doing everything and anything that's needed, so in a way this was counterintuitive."

For the first couple of months, there were many physician, nursing, and lean coaches at gemba to teach and ask questions wherever they saw that the process was not being followed. "Standard work and relentless coaching was the winning combination to hardwire the process," says Dr. MacKenzie.

Still, it was expected that at some point the system would get overwhelmed. Either too many patients would arrive at once or the back door (admissions boarding in the ED) would get clogged so that sicker patients could not move out of the ED. Eventually, any bottleneck in the system moves toward the front door and patients will end up back

---

25. Electronic medical record.

in the waiting room. This variability in demand in the ED required new thinking about how to escalate and de-escalate the new process.

"Given the variability of demand in the ED, a fixed system can too easily get overwhelmed," Kita says.

So, they created something like an andon system[26] and called it an escalation protocol. The protocol has five distinct levels that are triggered by specific demand and capacity targets. For each level there is standard work, by role, for what needs to be done, by whom. If a sudden surge of walk-in patients arrives at the ED and there are acute-care beds available in the back, for instance, the charge nurse systematically moves rapid-assessment candidates to the acute-care beds to temporarily relieve the surge. The escalation protocol is the playbook to inform everyone how to systematically change gears to meet a change in demand, says Kita.

In the end, this model cell yielded impressive results. Lehigh Valley avoided spending $18 million while serving a growing population. In the six months before implementation of the new system, in 2011, the Muhlenberg ED had to divert ambulances to other hospitals for approximately 50 hours each month. In the six months after, that number dropped to 20 hours. A month later, Muhlenberg began a run of 12 consecutive months with zero diversion hours.

The rapid-assessment unit has maintained an average of 26 minutes between the time a patient arrives and sees a provider. And the median length of stay for patients discharged from the ED dropped by 20 minutes while time-to-treatment decreased by 30 minutes.

---

26. Common to the Toyota Production System, andons are a system of visual cues—often in the form of red, yellow, or green lights high above a work station—that indicate what areas are working to the expected rate, which ones have issues, and where stoppages have occurred.

"Then a new surge in volume showed us that our ED is sometimes overfilling because we couldn't get patients admitted to the hospital, as there were no beds," Dale Lucht says. "We optimized the ED flow and then uncovered a flow issue downstream. We had lowered the water level and found our next big rock."[27] The work continues with new experiments being run all the time.

Much depends on this model cell, so it is important to learn the foundational elements of this work, including rapid-improvement events, 3P, and value-stream mapping. Good books have been written on these topics, so I will keep my descriptions short knowing that those who want to can find more depth elsewhere. Also, I should say that my knowledge and experience of these concepts all come by way of the Toyota Production System. If you know that some of the terms used are hot buttons within your organization and could create resistance, change the words but keep the meaning.

Rapid Improvement Events[28] involve the transformation of an existing process. This is when a cross-functional team of caregivers, executives, patients, technicians, and interested outsiders studies and then improves an area or work process, usually within a week or less. A rapid-improvement project can be one piece of a larger puzzle, or it can be aimed at a unique and troubling issue. The most common attributes of these events are that teams have stretch goals—nothing should be easy or rote—and are empowered to make necessary changes to achieve those goals. Teams report on their work, including a detailed statement of the problem, the root cause, and the countermeasure, but the point of

---

27. In lean systems, we refer to waste in processes as being like water that covers the rocks in a lake. As waste is removed, the water level drops and the real problems are exposed so that teams can address them.

28. For adherents of the Toyota Production System, this is equivalent to *kaizen,* a Japanese word that is widely translated as "change for the better." Many organizations have begun using English terms such as "continuous-improvement event" or "rapid-improvement event" in its place.

a rapid-improvement project is not to create a report. The goal is always to work together to make improvements.

Most projects shoot for reducing waste in a system or process by 50%. In the case of a model cell, 80% waste reduction is more appropriate. Teams need to stretch well past the typical improvement targets in order to reimagine the possible.

The *production preparation process,* or *3P,* is how a lean organization designs products and the work processes necessary to make those products. In healthcare, 3P is also used for major redesign or renovation projects, when many intersecting processes need to change together. The most important idea behind 3P is that teams working to meet the requirements of the customer will create processes with far less waste than if workflow is designed to suit internal needs.

For instance, I was a team member once on a 3P project to redesign workflows in a Labor and Delivery unit. Also on the team was a young mother whose son had a serious disease (Hirschsprung) that should have been diagnosed shortly after his birth. It was missed as the result of a broken process. The mother had graciously agreed to help us fix it, and so we were able to ask her, regarding every step in the mapped process, this critical question: "Would you pay for this?"

It may sound harsh in a healthcare setting, but this question strips a lot of extraneous noise from the question and focuses everyone on creating value instead of waste. Having this young mother in the room patiently telling us, for instance, that she would pay for us to administer medicine to her son (value) but not for the nurse to run down the hall to fetch the medicine from elsewhere (waste) was a powerful guide for our work. Having a centralized drug depot was convenient for us internally. But after running trials, it was also clear that those drug depots were the source of a lot of wasted time for nurses who ran back and forth.[29]

The patient's perspective is one of the important ways a team can identify what is *value creating*, what is *non–value creating* (and therefore should be eliminated), and what falls into the far trickier category of *necessary non–value creating*. For instance, most patients would absolutely pay for their diagnostic tests but would not want to pay to be wheeled all over the hospital to get that test. This traveling is non–value creating. However, we cannot yet wheel an MRI machine into a patient room. So, until the day that this breakthrough occurs, wheeling a patient three units over and one floor up to get an MRI is necessary but non–value creating.

Keeping a clear head about these distinctions is most important when teams begin creating *value-stream maps*. These are visual recordings of the patient-care process and information flow. First, teams create the current-state map, in which every step a patient takes through a particular care process is recorded. Then the team creates the future-state map, the step-by-step idealized path of a patient through that same process without waiting, waste, or errors.[30]

One of the best examples I have seen of using value-stream maps and 3P in a model cell takes us to Seattle Children's Hospital, where they were implementing lean ideas long before I had heard the phrase. Beginning in 1999, they were learning to do rapid-improvement events with lean experts from Boeing, starting with nonclinical areas, says Cara Bailey, senior vice president of Continuous Performance Improvement, or CPI.[31]

---

29. In the redesign, secure drug dispensers were placed in every patient room.

30. A sample value-stream map is in the appendix, figure 2.

31. Like some other healthcare organizations, Seattle Children's made a deliberate decision not to use the term "lean" to characterize their work in the beginning due to negative and often very narrow connotations some associate with the term.

So, by the time they were ready to plan a new outpatient surgery center in Bellevue, Washington, in 2007, they were confident that they could use the opportunity to completely redesign the flow of patient care using 3P.[32]

The business case for a new outpatient surgery center was simple. Additional capacity was needed, particularly in the Bellevue area east of Seattle, but the need was built on some complicated realities. As the academic and specialty medical referral center for a five-state region, Seattle Children's is a major teaching and research hospital, serving as the pediatric training site for the University of Washington. As such, the hospital receives a high number of complex cases. And both the numbers and complexity have been growing.

"Twenty years ago, we probably had 20% of patients in the ICU and 80% in regular units, but those numbers are flipping," says Dr. Lynn Martin, who is both director of the department of anesthesiology and medical director of CPI. "We're saving more babies, but they often become children with multiple issues. So our high-acuity cases that need ICU services have increased dramatically."

Hospital leadership decided to increase capacity and improve access to care on the main campus by moving common pediatric surgical procedures—fixing ear tubes, umbilical hernias, and circumcision, for example—to an outpatient facility in nearby Bellevue, Washington. The patients being treated there are all healthy enough to have an ambulatory procedure, leaving capacity for the more complicated cases at the main campus.

The cross-functional design team began by collecting feedback from families about their requirements for an outpatient center.[33] The team

---

32. At Seattle Children's, they refer to this 3P work as Integrated Facility Design.

33. The design team had a few core members and many others who shifted in and out of the team as needed, including providers, patients and families, architects, contractors, engineers, and administrative staff.

then identified seven distinct flows in an ambulatory surgical clinic: patients, family, providers, supplies, equipment, medication, and information. The "flows" were each like characters in a play. As directors, the team needed to understand the motives and intentions of each type of character and give them the simplest, most efficient path through their time on stage. Unlike live theater, however, the action was designed to produce the least amount of drama.

After collecting a lot of data about travel distances, safety hazards, and other issues based on the space in the main campus, the team started sketching out new ideas about the physical space with tabletop simulations. Then, armed with a lot of cardboard, tape, and markers, they took over a local warehouse and began simulating ideal work flows.

"We knew that families got confused when they were presented with a lot of different people," Dr. Martin says. "They come in with a child about to have surgery and it's not the best time to meet 15 new people with different titles and roles, all asking questions. And we all know that miscommunication is the greatest cause of harm."

So, they decided to cross-train nurses, who generally worked only in the OR, or postanesthesia recovery, or admitting, to take a patient all the way through. Three years after the surgery center opened, they were continuing to address issues and barriers while trying to execute this ideal plan.

The second pivotal decision the team made was that operating rooms, which are the most expensive piece of real estate in surgery centers, would be for surgery only. Nobody would wait in the OR while a patient fell asleep or woke up. This required working through a lot of details external to the operation and finding a way to match up lengthy prep work with short procedures and vice versa.

In the end, they constructed two small, peaceful induction rooms for each OR. Induction rooms all have two doors: one from the hallway and the other into surgery. Patients have a one-way looping journey: into the anesthesia room, then asleep and through the door into the OR, and then through another OR door that leads to private recovery rooms. Having two anesthesia rooms allows time for one patient to be falling asleep while next door another now–fully asleep patient is being wheeled into the OR ready for surgery. For procedures such as fixing a child's ear tube that can take just five minutes in surgery, having two anesthesia rooms feeding each OR has been pivotal to maintaining an even, consistent flow.

Teams also created aviation-style checklists on laminated cards, color-coded for the room (or stage of the procedure) that the patient was in. The checklists were crucial for nurses and anesthesia technicians because this is a one-way journey, for the sake of safe patient flow, with no opportunity for anyone to retrace his or her steps if an item is forgotten. The checklists assure that the team is taking all the patient-specific supplies and medications with the patient through the entire surgical journey.

Dr. Martin remained with the Bellevue surgical center through design, construction, and the first two years of operation before handing over the reins to Mark Reed, MD. Another anesthesiologist, Dr. Reed can lead you through a process so simple and elegant it can seem too easy.

"Seventy-two hours before surgery, a nurse calls the family to discuss the procedure, answer questions, and set their exact appointment time. We have everyone arrive here one hour before the procedure, and that timing is very important to our flow," Dr. Reed says. "Within 10 minutes of their arrival, the family is greeted and led back to anesthesiology. In the master plan, the nurse who greets the family is the one who called and answered questions 72 hours earlier and is the one who will be assisting in the OR."

With 14 full-time nurses on staff, only a small cohort can work the entire process so far, Dr. Reed acknowledges. Still, training continues, and working the whole process every time is a terrific goal.

Some of the youngest patients are not led back immediately but are encouraged to stay and play in the sunny, colorful waiting room so they can burn off a little more energy. There's a Starbucks café attached to the clinic waiting room downstairs from surgery and lots of activity areas, so it can get a little noisy there. Staff worried about noise levels initially, but family members assured them that they appreciated the sense of normalcy and community.

The patient and family are escorted to an induction room at a specific time, based on the anticipated length of preparation, so the child can be fully anesthetized as the previous surgery is ending. When the child is fully asleep, staff works through the checklist attached to the bed and then wheels the patient through the induction room's rear door and into the OR. Following surgery, the wheeled bed continues on through a private hall to a bank of recovery rooms where family joins the patient as he or she awakens.

Just behind the recovery rooms in a staff hallway are the oversized value-stream maps, detailing all the pieces of standard work involved in pediatric surgical flows, from presurgical consultation to "11.0 Conduct Post-Op Call." Any time staff members have a question about the way something happened, or should happen, the answers are here on big laminated posters marching down the hall.

Keep walking down this hallway, past the surgical and recovery areas, behind reception, and down the stairs and you will be in the building's busy ambulatory clinic, which was also designed using 3P. This is where more than 25 types of pediatric specialties see patients and families in a cleverly designed area meant to maximize provider communication. Imagine a doughnut. In the center of a ring of exam rooms is an open area of work stations—some desks at chair height, others designed for standing while working—for use by physicians, nurses, medical assistants, schedulers, and technicians. Patients arrive in the exam room through a door on the outside of the doughnut. As soon as a patient is seated, care providers are alerted and enter the exam room through a door on the doughnut's inside.

Flexible seating arrangements and the absence of private offices make for better communication between members of the care team, says Aaron Dipzinski, director of the Bellevue Clinic and Surgery Center. "We don't have assigned seating and, really, we don't want groups like surgeons or nurses to clump together," Dipzinski explains. "We want to avoid monuments and silos."

The result of all of this front-end attention to process has been remarkable. The Bellevue clinic opened in July 2011. In 2012, 2,704 surgeries were completed there. In 2013, the number increased to 3,137, and they expected to perform 3,300 surgeries in fiscal year 2014—the result of ongoing improvements to the work processes—making for 22% growth in output without increasing staff.

At the end of 2014, Dr. Reed and Dipzinski were beginning plans to open a third OR at Bellevue. With a well-designed process already in place, it was tempting, they admitted, to simply replicate the system, adjust staffing, and start doing one-third greater volume.

"But we know there are all kinds of improvements we can still make here," Dipzinski says. "There are efficiencies we've never dreamed of. So, we're thinking of slapping a clean sheet of paper over this first process map, getting new teams in here, and saying, 'Let's start fresh.'"

An experienced lean team like the one at Seattle Children's knows one important fact that every beginner must learn: the model cell does not exist in isolation. It represents one point in the total patient experience across time. You can have the best chemotherapy clinic in the nation, but if it is connected to a badly broken cancer unit, it will never be the optimized clinic you worked so hard for.

This is why it is important to start building an enterprise-wide value-stream map of the patient experience early, perhaps concurrently with the model cell. Make it visual so that people can stand in front of it and point to blockages and islands of excellence. Get everyone thinking about how the patient moves from one point of contact to the next and help to connect those dots into a seamless flow of care. When constructing the map for a cancer patient, for instance, that map will span five years of the patient's life. Chronic diseases such as diabetes demand a map that spans 50 years or more. That model cell that your team is rightfully proud of? How much space does it really occupy on the patient's value-stream map?

So, the work of the model cell is to break out and optimize one piece of the patient experience, one chewable chunk at a time. But remember that the model cell must eventually connect seamlessly with every other piece of the system.

Finally, let's look at a few things that both Lehigh Valley and Seattle Children's did to help their projects succeed. This is a list that every organization should incorporate into its standard work before beginning the controlled chaos that is a model cell.

In the planning stage, **select your team and target area for improvement carefully**. Begin with people who are truly interested in trying new things and who have a real investment in the targeted area. Leaders at Lehigh Valley needed a dynamic physician who was interested in new ideas. But more important, he was a trauma physician, well known and liked in the ED and capable of speaking everyone's language.

The results of the model cell should never be dependent on one physician or one personality, however. The team must have broad experience and be able to reflect the various needs and concerns of several groups. The fact that Seattle Children's found a second physician champion in Mark Reed, to take over from Lynn Martin, was important to their success.

Also, the team must **define what success looks like** before it begins. Members must collect all relevant data for the area and then decide which metrics are most important to their goals. It is critically important to understand how the existing process is performing. Collect baseline performance for several months before embarking on the model-cell work. Also be aware that there is almost always pressure to change what is being measured partway through the project as new facts are discovered. Choose at least one or two stable metrics that will show changes to quality or safety or cost over time. ThedaCare's Collaborative Care project team, for instance, chose medication reconciliation errors as a key metric to follow. At the beginning, our inpatient medical units were averaging a new error for every single patient admission. In the year after Collaborative Care was launched, there were zero such errors on the targeted units. No fancy spreadsheet could better show what the frontline teams were accomplishing.

This next item on the to-do list can be very challenging for some leaders: **let the teams make the decisions**. Give a team full agency to create and implement plans within the set guidelines and you will find that they are both more careful and more creative than they would have been with micromanaging oversight.

Set those teams free, but also be prepared to protect them from other parts of the organization with conflicting priorities if necessary. The model cell, with its strange ideas and different job descriptions, will be living in a hostile environment. This almost always causes tension between operations and support functions such as finance and HR, which are accustomed to controlling aspects of the work. There is a good chance that senior executives will be threatened by ideas that do not comply with existing bureaucratic rules. Senior leadership will need to smooth the path for the model cell.

If you can include leaders from finance or HR on some of the model-cell planning and improvement teams, that is ideal. At the very least, they need to be kept informed of the work's progress and have the opportunity to ask questions and offer input.

Bringing everyone along is, after all, one of the essential goals of any lean initiative. Not all of your people will want to go along. Resistance to change is inevitable. But everyone must be informed of what is happening and why and what the better future will look like—which is why we turn next to defining and communicating the values and principles that form the bedrock of this road.

3

Values
and Principles

Here are two words that get confused a lot: values and principles. The definitions get mixed up, turned around, and watered down until they are a well-meaning, flavorless gruel. And yet, what leaders truly believe (values) and the rules or policies they espouse (principles) are critically important to a lean culture. So, let's lay out some clear definitions and describe actions you can take to underscore and promote lean values and principles.

Values are a person's deeply held and chosen beliefs. These are not inherited prejudices or whimsical notions. Values are a reflection of who a person chooses to be and what he or she judges to be important in this life. Values color every decision a person makes. A leader who believes deeply in the restorative and creative value of fun will create a very different organization from one who believes that only a steady and somber hand should guide the plow.

Establishing a core set of values is critical to shaping a desirable culture. At ThedaCare, we spoke often of our values—courage to speak the truth, joy in our work, thirst for learning—in order to create an environment where it was safe to identify and solve problems every day.

Principles are how a person or a team organizes and externalizes values. In the way that values drive the culture, principles drive behaviors. For instance, the first-stated principle of a lean organization is respect for people. To show this principle in behavior, lean organizations declare that no person will lose his or her job due to continuous improvement and productivity improvements.

Principles can also help people find points of common ground with others. Most people work with others who share some but not all of their values. Some people are deeply spiritual, for instance, and need to work closely with nonbelievers. In a thoughtful organization, these two groups can find common ground in shared principles, even when a few personal values are very different.

For inspiration on this issue, I often find myself turning to Paul O'Neill, the CEO of Alcoa mentioned in the introductory chapter. The world's largest aluminum producer and miner of bauxite, Alcoa had suffered from management missteps for years before O'Neill took over in 1987. Investors were nervous, and company morale was low. O'Neill needed to prove very quickly that he had the right vision for the business. What he told Wall Street was that employee safety was his focus and that safety, not financial statements or return on investment, was the metric by which he should be judged. This was not what anyone expected to hear.

For many years before taking on Alcoa, however, O'Neill had been making lists and thinking deeply about what kind of leader he should be. He wanted to dig down into what was truly important and kept coming back to people. While every annual report says something along the lines of "People are our most valuable resource," O'Neill says he wanted to lead an organization where that was verifiably true.

For O'Neill, establishing a goal of zero workplace injuries was the very best way to say that employees are valuable. He strongly believed in showing respect for people and made it into a principle for his organization by declaring that worker safety was the top priority for everyone. How did he put that into action? Constantly.

One day, for instance, he was in a smelting plant in Alcoa, Tennessee, meeting with all employees in the same room. As he did in every location, he told the group that safety was everyone's first concern. He said, "If there is ever a situation where you feel this plant is unsafe and the problem is not being attended to effectively, I want you to call me." Then he wrote his home phone number on the blackboard.

A few weeks later, he received a call at 11 p.m. from a worker in Tennessee who had just come on shift. As O'Neill recounted several years later during a meeting of chief executives in Pittsburgh, the man said, "You said to call you if there were unsafe conditions so here goes. One section of the roller conveyor system for moving ingots from the casting pit to the rolling mill has been broken for three days. So six or seven of us have to pick up these 600-pound ingots and move them across the broken section and we are concerned we are going to be badly injured."

O'Neill thanked the man and said he would attend to it immediately. He called the plant manager at home, got him out of bed, and told him the story. Then he asked the plant manager to go down to the plant immediately and start working on a solution to the broken pulley. O'Neill said, "And call me when it is fixed."

As O'Neill describes it, the "tom-tom communication" system at the plant started booming. A frontline worker had called the CEO at home at 11 p.m. about a safety problem and it was fixed within a few hours. That was just one example of many.

Values that you hold in your heart or principles written on a piece of paper in the boardroom mean nothing until they are modeled. O'Neill made his values and principles real to every single one of the 60,000 workers at Alcoa. And when he left Alcoa in 2000, the number of lost days due to accidents had fallen from 1.87 per 100 workers to 0.2. (Alcoa was a lot larger and more profitable, too.)

Leaders need to craft principles that are useful for the path ahead while still speaking to the existing culture. That might sound like a tall order. Fortunately, there is a great starting point in the lean principles that were established by the Shingo Prize.

Shigeo Shingo was a teacher and industrial engineer who worked with many Toyota Motor Company suppliers and taught the tools of the Toyota Production System around the world. When he retired, professors at the school of business at Utah State University established an institute and a prize in his honor, which every year is awarded to companies who score very high on a rigorous on-site examination. Leaders at the school also used Shingo's writing and teaching to identify the principles of a lean organization. These nine doctrines work as well in healthcare as they do in manufacturing or in any company that is seeking a culture of continuous improvement and sustainable excellence. I highly recommend that organizations adopt these principles and use them to guide daily decisions.

Respect every individual. Real respect for people means working to keep everyone safe from harm, listening to and encouraging ideas and initiatives, and giving people the training and freedom to fix the problems they encounter.

O'Neill, who also helped found the Pittsburgh Regional Health Initiative, says that he gauges respect by whether the people in a company can say yes to these three statements, every day:

1. I am treated with dignity and respect by everyone without regard to pay level or title or race, ethnicity, gender, or any other qualifying condition.

2. I am given the things I need—tools, training, encouragement— to make a contribution to this organization in a way that gives meaning to my life.

3. I am recognized for what I do by someone I care about.[34]

If all leaders used these statements to judge their organizations, companies would be managed very differently. Think for a moment about that second statement. To make it true, a person's work would have value not just for the organization but also for the individual. A person could not be assigned to do wasteful, repetitive, or non-value-creating work. It would be disrespectful.

Another way that people are disrespected, perhaps unwittingly, is when initiatives and projects are piled on, leaving them with a sense that little can be accomplished against a mountain of needs. I see this all the time. In a hospital in North Carolina, for instance, I asked a hospital's 17 top executives to name every critical initiative that they were tracking. I gave them pads of yellow sticky notes and said, "One initiative per note."

At the end of 15 minutes, those executives had 222 sticky notes plastered over the walls of that conference room. Guess who was going to do that work required by those initiatives—gathering data, researching various possibilities? I can tell you it was not those executives. Launching new initiatives is easy; it gives us the illusion that something positive is about to happen. Subtracting them requires hard work, honest debates, and— there's no other word for it—leadership.

---

34. Jerry Bussell, *Anatomy of a Lean Leader* (UL LLC., 2012) 93

Healthcare organizations beginning a lean journey must learn to focus their initiatives to the critical few, all of which must be aligned with the organization's top metrics, also known as True North. Healthcare organizations have hundreds of metrics that must be followed and reported to governments and other organizations. This creates a cacophony and much confusion as to what really matters. As senior leaders, our job is to create clarity in the face of this chaos. So, deselecting metrics, initiatives, and special programs becomes as important as selecting them.

I often tell teams that the way to winnow the projects is to keep those sticky notes up on the wall and, for the first year, make a pledge to add no new initiatives. During this time, the wall also needs to be decluttered by terminating extraneous projects.

And for every new initiative begun, there should be a plan for when and how to abandon it. There must be dates for reassessment and milestones to pass to keep the initiative alive. If the project fails at the milestones, is it worth your time? When the team decides to stop work on a failing project and you can tell an employee, "We've decided that your time is more valuable than this initiative," you will be showing real respect.

Most of us can begin showing this kind of respect immediately. Review the workload of one of your direct reports. In an in-depth conversation, find out whether there are dead-end projects on his or her list of worries. Work to remove them.

Lead with humility. CEOs and other leaders are not generally rewarded for being humble. In most cases, it is the opposite. Leaders are expected—by themselves and others—to have all the answers. And it feels great to step onto that pedestal and make the solutions rain down.

No one person has all the answers, however, and humility demands that we recognize this. As an internist, a medical director, and then a CEO, I was rarely if ever the one who got his hands dirty investigating problems and experimenting with solutions. I did not even know what the real problems were. My staff knew more than I did, but they did not know all the issues and answers, either. Everyone in an organization has but pieces of the whole picture.

The idea might be difficult for some to accept, but in humility there is great freedom. We can stop pretending to know everything. We can walk through our hospitals without offering lectures. A humble leader is someone who goes to the front line and asks questions, seeking to help where he or she can. Instead of shooting from the hip and feeling that pedestal wobble under his or her feet, the lean leader asks for input from others.

For most of us, humility is a learned behavior. The first time I went to gemba, I was nervous. Although I had practiced medicine for many years, spending time on the front line as CEO was quite different. I did not know what to do or what to say to the people who would be staring at me. I read management books describing "walk-arounds," which meant exactly that: wandering around and saying hello. Was I supposed to be a politician now, pressing the flesh and kissing babies?

My sensei described something quite different. My purpose on the floor, he said, was to go and look for problems. More accurately, I was learning to see the problems that our employees faced every day in trying to deliver perfect care to our patients. I needed to see the problems and then learn how to help remove the barriers. Please note: I was not there to solve the problems. I was there to help facilitate the solutions that they—the front line—would find.

The fact that I did not know how to do this lean work, and that I had to learn it in front of others, was humbling for me. I was no longer the man with all the answers who was locked away in the nice office. I was human and fallible, and, at gemba, I learned how to be useful.

No matter whether you are a CEO or a midlevel manager, it requires humility to go to gemba and admit that you do not have all the answers and that you are willing to learn how patient care (or value) is actually being delivered. Incorporating humble practices like this will help any leader begin to live this principle.

Here is how you start: On Monday morning, go to gemba and watch how work is being done. Ask respectful and open-ended questions about what you are seeing. Ask how you can help. Look for ways you can uniquely contribute, such as smoothing over a problem with a disgruntled doctor or making sure the nurse has all the resources required to care for her critically injured patient. Thank your colleagues for their work and for the time they spend answering your questions. It is an exercise that can take 10 or 15 minutes out of your day and, over time, it can change everything.

Seek perfection. Everyone values life; doing so is practically a condition of being alive. But how does this bedrock value translate into a principle? Lean leaders show they value life by seeking perfection: the absolute zero. That means aiming for zero preventable mortalities, zero infections due to treatment, zero minutes that a patient has to spend waiting for treatment.

Seeking perfection does not mean expecting the organization to arrive at perfection anytime soon. Instead, organizations embrace perfection as a principle in order to be reminded on a daily basis that the goal is not *OK* or *good enough* but flawless healthcare delivery.

Chase perfection, but beware of falling prey to perfectionism. There is a strong strain of perfectionism, pedantry, and nitpicking that runs through healthcare. Many of us fear making change without being guaranteed of the outcome. Colleagues will argue adamantly that no change should be made unless it has been proved both necessary and incapable of failure five times over. But seeking perfection means chasing after that zero, always trying new ideas and methods to get closer. Perfect is the goal, but never let it get in the way of better.

Healthcare leaders especially need to chase that zero because every day in this business the lives of our fellow human beings are at stake. In 2010, the Department of Health and Human Services released a study showing that 13.5% of all Medicare beneficiaries experienced harm during hospitalization that was the fault of bad practices. Further, the HHS Inspector General found that mistakes contributed to the deaths of 15,000 patients every month.[35] The American public seems to accept this terrible performance with barely a murmur, and that amazes me. I cannot believe this complacency will last much longer.

If the goal were zero preventable deaths, a good target would be a 50% improvement every year. Some years, an organization might reduce preventable deaths by 30% or 35%. This is terrific improvement, even if the target was not met. Still, the goal remains zero.[36] To get a little closer to the goal every day, to arrive at better on the way to zero, focus on creating systems and health delivery processes without room for errors.

To begin, choose a real business problem that is rooted in one of the four main categories: safety, quality, delivery, or cost. The problem should be easily stated in a sentence, must be a significant business issue, and must be measurable. In other words, if your business problem is that you are facing lawsuits after three patients suffered significant injuries from falling out of bed, do not say that your goal is zero lawsuits (no matter how tempting). Safety is the issue, so you select the most common injury

---

35. Daniel R. Levinson, "Adverse Events in Hospitals: National Incidence among Medicare Beneficiaries," Office of the Inspector General, Department of Health and Human Services (2010)

36. When ThedaCare set the target to halve preventable deaths every year, they scored 100 on the Hospital Standardized Mortality Ratio, which was the national average. Fewer than 10 years later, the score was 50, meaning that preventable mortality was reduced by half.

type—patient falls, for instance—and begin by measuring how many falls happen every day.

On Monday morning, announce that the organization will be reducing patient falls by 50% over the next year. Set a process in place to document every patient fall and keep track of every report. A cross-functional team should be tasked with finding common reason for the falls and making changes to keep patients safe. Make sure to relinquish control to the team while supporting their efforts and keeping watch over how targets are being met. If patient falls are reduced by redefining "patient falls," for instance, nothing is accomplished. When you seek perfection by finding root causes and solutions, you begin to chase zero.

Ensure quality at the source. In manufacturing, this lean principle is about making mistakes visible and not allowing them to move ahead in the system. It means that a poorly shaped widget will be identified and removed from production as soon as possible.

In healthcare, ensuring quality at the source also means being able to quickly identify errors and stop them from causing more damage down the line. This means that systems are in place to alert caregivers about harmful drug interactions, for instance, or to ensure that diagnostic testing is completed and reviewed in a timely fashion.

Building quality into care delivery processes often means creating tollgates at critical junctures. These are decision points in the patient's journey where teams have written standard work for staff to check that particular things have happened and to verify that the patient is responding appropriately before any more time passes.

For instance, when a pneumonia patient is admitted to a medical unit at ThedaCare, a clock in the system begins running. Within 90 minutes, the lead nurse is notified to check that the hospitalist, nurse, pharmacist, and social worker have conducted their initial bedside meeting with patient and family to create a plan of care. Ninety minutes later, the nurse checks the patient's oxygen saturation level. If it is not 90% or better, the nurse follows a course of standard work that helps him study the problem and make adjustments.

In this way, teams build care processes that bring quality problems to the surface while creating standardized responses in order to discover what works and what does not.

To begin: once you have identified that important business problem you are addressing, you will probably need to admit that you do not know how the work that underlies this problem is performed. Most organizations will find that they have something like 300% variation in how tasks are performed, no matter how critical or basic. So, set to work with a team at mapping every aspect of the processes that make up this work, from the time each step takes, to who completes the task, to the number of times the step produces defects.

Once you understand the present state, you will be able to see where mistakes are made and where the process is prone to breakdown. Ensure that teams that are creating these maps receive instruction on these concepts and then demonstrate how they are ensuring quality at the source. You will most likely need an external sensei to do the teaching, since building quality at the source is still a foreign concept in most of healthcare delivery.

Scientific thinking. Most of us learned the plan-do-study-act (PDSA) cycle of scientific thinking in high school science courses. It is the fundamental principle underlying medical science today. But do we practice scientific thinking in our daily decision making? Or do we coast along assuming that science is just somehow magically embedded in everything or is applicable only in laboratory conditions?

It is my observation that healthcare professionals make a lot of assumptions about work processes. Caregivers assume that someone else has used scientific thinking to establish, test, and validate the work processes. Leaders tend to believe that people will ask the right questions when things go wrong. It is time to challenge these assumptions.

In order to be a highly reliable healthcare delivery system, everyone must employ PDSA in designing processes and in solving every problem encountered in operating those processes. This involves everyone. From the president of the hospital to a pharmacy technician, everyone must instinctively use PDSA thinking when confronted with problems.

Two things are getting in the way of widespread PDSA thinking. First, people are so accustomed to specialization they often assume that someone else has the job of checking decisions against facts and sound analysis. That is what the quality department does, right? But if scientific thinking belongs only to the few and frontline workers are not empowered to think and act scientifically, they end up kicking problems up the chain of command and then waiting 60 days for the recommendations of a committee. By contrast, when everyone reflexively uses scientific thinking, problems are addressed immediately.

Second, if people use PDSA at all, they usually stop halfway. In healthcare, people do a lot of planning and doing but neglect to study what happens and then adjust procedures. Hospitals and clinics are wastelands of half-finished projects and data that people really meant to analyze last month. *Plan* and *do* are fun. But in *study* and *adjust* are the real discoveries that help us reshape patient care. This is where people learn about what is working and what is not.

Physicians are taught to use PDSA in the diagnosis and treatment of patients but usually don't extended scientific thinking to the system that is delivering care to patients. Doing the latter is the essence of continuous improvement and lean healthcare.

To begin instilling a PDSA reflex throughout your organization, you will need to bring in a coach or sensei because this is a new reflex. You will know you have the right coach when he or she insists that you can learn only by doing. With a coach, begin working systematically through an important business problem by applying PDSA thinking to every step. Learn to work through an A3,[37] but remember that this work is not about filling out forms. It is about chasing zero.

Focus on process. Every system is a series of processes perfectly designed to deliver the results that it does, whether or not the design was conscious and intentional. From long years of observation, people in lean healthcare know that errors are almost always caused by badly designed processes, not by people. Frontline caregivers are harmed (and embarrassed) over and again when they are blamed for mistakes that are hardwired in the process. Meanwhile, patients are harmed over and over again.

For most healthcare organizations, *focus on process* will mean clearly defining the process from end to end—for example, medication reconciliation, catheter removal, admitting patients to a unit from the ED—and establishing standard work for every step. Standard work is a team's best current thinking on how work should be done. After every improvement project, team members write out the revised step-by-step process for performing tasks. Standard work is then audited for ongoing effectiveness and changed only by a team's agreement.

---

37. The A3 is a more detailed version of the plan-do-study-act process defined by W. Edwards Deming. It is a standardized form showing the scientific method for problem solving on a single sheet of A3 paper, including the business context and possible root causes for the problem. A sample is in the appendix, figure 3.

Those of us in lean healthcare do this work because we know that we cannot improve what we cannot see and measure. Only when we know how a task is being performed every time can we know whether that method is effective and how it might effect upstream and downstream processes.

For some people, standard work will still sound like handcuffs or "cookbook medicine." So it is helpful to talk about the pieces of standard work that people already do every day. People return their toothbrushes and utensils to the same place after every use, for instance, because nobody wants to waste time repeatedly searching for the same items.

Howard Jeffries, a pediatrician at Seattle Children's Hospital, likes to describe standard work as a mechanism to set people free. He is right. Practitioners would rather treat a patient than search frantically for the right tools or medicines to treat the patient. With standard work, we free the practitioner's mind from thinking about a lot of repetitive, mundane tasks. When there is just one way to do simple tasks and everyone knows it, minds are free to focus on anomalies or changes in the patient's condition. This is where real value lies.

This means systems must be in place to train people in the standard work that exists for every job they transfer to. And teams need to learn how to write standard work for and with the frontline caregivers performing the tasks. When everyone is involved in creating, following, and observing standards, it is less likely that people will feel handcuffed or that their autonomy is being infringed upon. It becomes clear that everyone is in it together.

Standard work is the single most important tool to help an organization shift from a culture of shame and blame to one that focuses on process, on rooting out the bad work sequences and improving flow. The goal is to build a culture where people feel safe to expose problems.

To begin creating standard work in your organization, go to gemba and ask questions about how the work in a given process is being accomplished. Then ask, *How should the work be accomplished?* The people doing the work generally know where the problems in the existing process are. When asked for opinions, people doing the work can usually articulate the problems and offer improvement ideas. Thank people for their time and insight. Thank them for pointing out problems and errors.

When Mike Hoseus, coauthor of the seminal book *Toyota Culture*, began working at Toyota Motor Manufacturing in Kentucky, he was first sent to the assembly line. Hoseus was on track to become general manager, but first he needed to learn the work. He was given training and a drill and put on the line. Within a matter of hours, he managed to scratch the wheel well with his drill. He stopped, looked hard at that andon light, and wondered whether to pull it and stop the line. It was such a rookie error. Maybe nobody would see the scratch. But, as Hoseus tells the story, his training kicked in and he pulled that cord and stopped the line.

For two minutes, he stalled production in the plant while a supervisor inspected the damage and showed Hoseus the proper way to hold his drill. By the time cars were moving again, Hoseus says, he was dreading lunch. He was not sure whether his colleagues would be angry or make fun of him, but he was pretty sure it would not be pleasant. At lunch, the plant president came into the break room and, in front of everyone, shook Hoseus' hand. He said, "Hoseus-san, thank you for finding this error."

Imagine if a hospital president came to the gemba and sincerely thanked someone for bringing forward a medication error. It would be a significant step toward changing the culture.

Think systemically. Many problems in healthcare are the result of not a single process but many processes that affect each other. To address these problems, leaders need to consider the whole system—all the interactions and intersections, planned or accidental.

At ThedaCare, for instance, we did an analysis of the cancer value stream, meaning every aspect of care that we give cancer patients in their five-year journeys, and it showed that only 35% of the care delivered to breast cancer patients was delivered in facilities owned by ThedaCare. Also, ThedaCare employed only about 20% of the caregivers.

Our service to these fragile patients was, by definition, fragmented. No one was looking at the whole value stream from start to finish. It should surprise no one that this fractured process with poorly connected steps across organizations was a root cause for many defects that patients experienced. Handoffs were mismanaged. Appointments and follow-ups were neglected. Patients were left unsure and were sometimes misdirected.

Instead, try to think about care delivery systems the same way that physicians think about treating their patients' bodies. Every part of the organism is important; if one part is optimized at the expense of other parts, the whole system suffers.

Here is a simple rule for helping to keep the whole system in mind: patients are the center of the universe. Everyone is organized around creating value for the customer. The walls created between work silos— between units, physician groups, and subspecialties—must fall in the face of patient needs and their journeys through medical care.

Lean leaders must be system leaders, thinking of the organization as one organism with all functions interdependent and in balance to deliver the best result for patients. All of the organs must function in harmony.

That will require multidisciplinary teams that focus on whole-system problems. This is the only way to deliver a perfect patient experience.

To begin: Gather a team and begin creating a map of one patient's journey through your hospital or clinic. Note every interaction and how information follows the patient. Look for places where your siloed operations get in the way of a seamless patient experience, and start talking about how to deconstruct those walls. Then, as you make progress within your walls, start to look at the value stream as it flows through other organizations that encounter the customer earlier—perhaps in an independent primary care group—and later, after being released from your hospital.

Create constancy of purpose. Creating value for the patient is the organization's purpose, and that must be the oft-repeated message in a lean environment. It is the reason behind every rapid-improvement event, every piece of standard work, and every True North metric.

Value is always defined from the patient's perspective. This is why, whenever leaders and improvement teams have the opportunity, they need to ask patients: "Would you pay for that if you had a choice?" It is humbling to find out how much of what healthcare does *to* or *for* patients has no value in their eyes. Part of your purpose should be to remove all non-value-creating steps in all care processes. By doing this, you will be able to see and remove waste such as defects, waiting time, and overutilization to lower cost and improve quality.

Constancy of purpose also means keeping the direction focused and priorities in line. Lean is an operating system,[38] and within that system there are many moving parts. Leaders remain focused by keeping the moving parts—big projects and strategic initiatives—to a minimum.

---

38. An operating system is a series or set of programs defined by specific rules that function interdependently and govern all activities of an organization. Think of the operating system on every computer or mobile device as a near equivalent.

Every healthcare organization has strategic initiatives. When I was CEO of ThedaCare, we had 33 strategic initiatives and thought we were brilliant for having come up with so many. When we began implementing lean, however, I heard from a lot of midlevel managers that they were drowning in work. They had improvement projects to follow up and strategic initiatives to push and no time to worry about patients.

So we took a hard look at what we were doing and found a lot of the old management by objective. For every strategic initiative, such as "Grow the cardiac service line by 5% over the next year," we gave managers a list of tactics to follow. We might say, go talk to every cardiac provider in a 100-mile radius and all the ambulance drivers, too. Nobody was suggesting that the manager look hard at our current state first. Instead of providing better value to patients, our managers were chasing tactics.

Our message was confusing and stressful but not unique. In most organizations, managers spend 80% of their time working on strategic initiatives and just 20% of their time helping the front line. Now, I tell organizations to limit their strategic initiatives to a critical few—fewer than five—and make sure that everyone knows how those initiatives are tied to the True North metrics.[39]

Strategic initiatives should also speak to the hearts and minds of your people. Think about why people come to work in healthcare every day. What are their highest aspirations for their patients and community? They probably do not include growing the cardiac service line by 5%. True North and strategic initiatives alike should be a clarion call to

---

39. The right mix, I believe, happens when managers and executives spend 20% of organizational resources on strategic initiatives and 80% on improving value at the front line. If every executive is focused on spending 80% of resources at the front line, frontline workers will be able to pull resources from every department—HR, finance, IT, improvement system—to solve problems immediately.

action: to save lives, to improve health, and to ensure that patients (and our organizations) are not bankrupted in the process.

To begin: Count your pet projects and strategic initiatives. Start a conversation about how to winnow these to a manageable few.

Transparency through visual management. For many people, this will be an unsettling principle to live. This involves tracking and displaying all errors and improvement efforts on large boards for everyone to see. Remember: people cannot fix what they cannot see. Visual management is used to make improvement opportunities both visible and difficult to forget.

There are two important parts of visual management to keep in mind. The visual part is about putting data on public display to make sure that everyone is seeing facts, not rumors or speculation. The management part is where you do something about it.

Every hospital that implements visual management begins the effort with a certain amount of dread. "Patients will see our mistakes" is a common worry. It is true that patients will see data on your errors. But your faults are not news to them. The patients who do stop to study your visual management boards will learn that you are diligently working on improvements. That will be the real headline news.

At SickKids Hospital in Toronto, for instance, visual management boards in a hallway of the pediatric medicine unit show the most up-to-date data on infections and medication errors. This is available for anyone to see, and it is not unusual for members of staff to have conversations with parents in front of those boards as they explain what they are doing to combat common hospital infections and errors. This level of honesty means that everyone is accountable to the patient, which is as it should be.

To begin practicing transparency through visual management, create a mock-up of your calendar for the next month that is large enough to be easily seen by your whole team and include every meeting and function you attend. With a team—because everyone needs to learn how to do this—ask which of these meetings are value creating for the customer. Put a red dot on every meeting or function that is not adding value.

This is not just a public statement of waste. It is also a way to begin having conversations around value and waste in your daily life. Every time someone wants to add a meeting onto your calendar, show him your red dots and ask, "Which category does this meeting fall under? Is it another red dot?" If it is, do not add it.

Using these principles will make hard decisions a little easier because they are your guideposts. For every question ask, Is this what a respectful organization does? Will this show that we are seeking perfection? Is this the action of an organization based on scientific thinking?

To keep all of these principles alive and active as guides, we must create an infrastructure that rewards adherence to lean healthcare while creating lean teachers and facilitators. And so next, we begin creating your central improvement team.

4

The Central
Improvement Team

Fitting an old organization with a new operating system is a risky procedure. Careers rise and fall based on what happens during the transition. Organizations that are successful will feel heroic; failure can undermine the confidence of an entire health system. Leaders whom I have met on the cusp of a transition all want to know the same thing: how can I make sure this will work?

My answer is to make a strong, succinct case for change that is easy for everyone to understand. Make sure your message is focused on the patient. Educate yourself and all your top executives in lean thinking. And then reshape the career expectations of managers and executives around continuous improvement. Lean healthcare organizations do this with a centralized improvement team that usually reports to the CEO.

The central improvement team is called by many names—lean promotion office, performance improvement team, etc.—but it should always be the repository of lean expertise and a path for promotion. The systems that I believe are most effective feature two-year rotations through the central improvement team for people who are seen as leaders with potential. Team members get trained in lean skills and then lead or assist in improvement projects throughout the organization. This way, every leader eventually has a solid background in lean thinking and has worked throughout the organization. Also, acquiring lean skills becomes part of a promotion instead of a burden or an academic exercise.

Think of the improvement team as the bloodstream of an organization. People move through the team acquiring knowledge the way that blood acquires oxygen. These new lean thinkers are then spread through the organization and bring a specific kind of energy to the front line.

So the purpose of this team is threefold: to facilitate lean activities while teaching lean concepts and to develop the health system's future leaders. At ThedaCare, there are now 100 executives, managers, and supervisors who were once lean facilitators. From this experience we have learned that when management is deeply entrenched in lean thinking, the culture moves quicker in the right direction.

Everyone on the team should be full-time, with no other duties. It is my experience that other duties will always trump improvement efforts, if allowed. In addition, potential leaders from throughout the organization, including support services such as finance and human resources, should be encouraged to seek positions on the central improvement team. All parts of the organization will be using the same operating system, after all, so it is important that everyone uses the same language and has the same goals.

This is also your opportunity to unify all improvement efforts. Most health systems have one or two—or a half-dozen—improvement efforts under way. Maybe a couple of people are still working through a GE 90-day Workout, while one division is trying for a Baldrige National Quality Award and another division is invested heavily in Six Sigma.

All of these efforts must now come under the central improvement team office.

This can be done respectfully, with certain aspects of other programs being incorporated into lean healthcare. But the leader who leaves orphan improvement programs out there to slowly die by neglect risks a tide of resentment from people who put real effort into those now-sidelined programs. The leaders of your central improvement team should recognize the commonalities between lean healthcare and other initiatives by focusing on the principles from the previous chapter and then make a plan for creating a unified effort.

Your organization may also need to more clearly define roles and duties in some support services. The quality department will likely still need to collect and report data to the government or various agencies, and it may make sense to retain clinical improvement training in this department. This department will coordinate closely with the central improvement team, however, as all the principles and tools will be standardized under the one central improvement office.

How big the central improvement team should be and how its members should learn lean thinking are matters of some debate. My experience is that 1% of FTEs on the team is sufficient. Slip too far below this number and you run the risk of a marginalized lean team with sluggish circulation.

When the ThedaCare Improvement System was just getting started with our lean office, I picked out 12 of our best people and called each one to offer the job. They came from frontline management, from various improvement roles, and from the front line of care. We were about to radically change ThedaCare, I told each one, and I wanted him or her to help me lead the charge. I promised support and that good opportunities would await them on the other side. The senior VP of quality and human resources led the team and directly reported to me so that everyone understood the CEO was taking a personal interest. Every one of my recruits agreed to join.[40]

So, I had my team. But how were we going to get them ready to lead large and small improvement projects, to create value-stream maps and 3P laboratories? Here is another fork in the road with two valid paths to take. Let's call the paths Training Wheels and Inside Expert.

The Training Wheels approach involves finding the right lean consulting group that can train your team while leading rapid-improvement events. This is what I chose to do at ThedaCare. Outside consultants were out at gemba every week for the first six years, training and leading different kinds of projects. As the lean team's skills increased, members became mentors and taught lean skills throughout the organization.

When frontline consultants are no longer needed, the training wheels come off. Many organizations retain an external sensei for years after to help leaders see hidden issues. But it is important that everyone knows from the beginning—and prepares for the day—that your organization will own this work.

Helen Macfie has a classic example of this method in action, with a couple of interesting twists. Now the chief transformation officer of MemorialCare in Southern California, Macfie was the vice president of performance improvement in 2006 when she helped lead MemorialCare's six-hospital system down a lean path. They did not call it "lean" at first because they feared it would sound too much like the next big cost-cutting initiative, she says, but they were introduced to lean thinking by some of the masters: Seattle Children's Hospital, Virginia Mason Medical Center, and Boeing.

---

40. Over time, the office grew to a maximum of 36 people—about 1% of ThedaCare's FTEs— and then dropped back down to a lower number. As more fully trained lean experts rotated out of the office and into leadership roles, we needed fewer facilitators.

Macfie knew she needed help to get started, so she began interviewing consulting firms. She and her team listened to consultants describe their training methods and their recommendations on where and how to begin. They knew they had found the right match when a Washington State consultant group talked about time horizons.

"Their idea was that they would be with us for about five years and then we would get a friendly divorce," Macfie says. "That made sense to us since consulting is so expensive and we really wanted to grow our own expertise and capacity."

Their journey began cautiously. That first year they did 17 improvement events, which they called proof-of-concept tests, primarily at the 313-bed acute-care Saddleback Memorial Medical Center in Laguna Hills. Macfie, along with her "partner in crime" Tamra Kaplan, created a central improvement office with just two other interested people and a part-time secretary to keep them organized.

As they gained confidence, they moved into other facilities and began differentiating projects. Rapid Process Improvements and 5S[41] were four- or five-day team events where the results were expected to be implemented on the following Monday. Rapid Process Design events were "for the more gnarly road-map projects." The team initially looked for big-impact improvements that would help tell the story of lean. One event at Long Beach Memorial Medical Center and Miller Women's and Children's Hospital, for instance, helped them avoid the $750,000 cost of a fourth digital mammography machine yet moved patients through the process quicker and cut down on wait time. A lot of people in the organization learned about lean thinking by touring the mammography unit at the Friday report-out and hearing that story.

---

41. Popularized by the Toyota Production System and based on five Japanese words that begin with "s," 5S focuses on cleaning, organizing, and standardizing the workplace. The five Ss can be translated into English as sort, separate, shine, standardize, and sustain.

During year two of the journey, they did 47 events, and by year three, they were doing 80–100 events per year and were looking for additional improvement facilitators, whom they call "lean fellows," for their newly christened Lean Resource Office. Macfie and Kaplan created criteria for the job of fellow, developed a list of names, and asked the chief operating officers of the various hospitals and divisions for input. It was not always perfect.

In the beginning, new fellows were asked for two-year commitments and spent their first 18 months in training. It was an intensive program, testing a fellow's analytical and leadership skills and his or her ability to rapidly assimilate new information and facilitate projects through to completion. Not everyone was able to finish the training, and it was difficult, though absolutely necessary, to integrate those people who did not make the level of fellow back into their old job or another without a loss of status or respect. Also, fellows who completed training and left after two years gave back little time to the lean office. Most fellows came back to the lean team for short periods each year to stay current on techniques and lean facilitation skills and to lead teams. Still, the training-to-facilitating ratio was out of balance.

As Macfie's friendly divorce from the original consultants approached in year 5, she and her team took over and streamlined the lean fellow training into a 12-month program, followed by 12 months of full-time facilitation. They created additional training for the advanced position of master fellow and became more skilled at assessing potential fellows.

Some people who join the lean office are lifers, Macfie says. They are dedicated, love the energy, and do not mind the sometimes-long hours and hard work. But most fellows end up staying with the office for about five years. Those who go back into nursing or pharmacy or other sections return at a higher level and bring lean thinking into their new jobs. Tamra Kaplan, for instance, was promoted to COO for Long

Beach Memorial after three years running the Lean Resource Office and was succeeded by Brian Stuckman, now VP for materials and lean resources, and Lorra Browne, master fellow and director of the Lean Resource Office.

Seven years into their lean journey, MemorialCare had a lean office consisting of 10 fellows, three data analysts, and an office coordinator, with plans for new hires to staff the transformation at newly acquired organizations. To expand capacity in the facilitator ranks, they also created tracks for an additional six fellows who remain in their frontline jobs and may rotate through the Lean Resource Office only occasionally. These are called embedded fellows. To grow expertise of line managers and leadership, they developed a four-day lean management training program that includes mandatory completion of a project. That program has graduated more than 400 managers so far, including many physicians. Of those, about 80 have gone on to a higher "certified lean leader" level where they can co-lead workshops, run events and A3s, provide coaching, and serve as role models.

"We had to make sure that managers knew more than their people about running improvement projects," Macfie says, "so they can foster the work of the event teams, introduce daily management, and strengthen their coaching skills for the long haul."

With 11,700 employees in the MemorialCare system, the Lean Resource Office is still well shy of the 1% mark. However, Macfie says they are continuing on with steady growth as the system grows and continuing to train managers, lean leaders, and embedded fellows.

"For us, a lesson learned has been that having a planned divorce was really good. Tensions will naturally grow between consultants and clients as you evolve your own lean expertise and style, and it was good to have that plan in place and to be ready to make the leap on our own," Macfie says.

"Now, at the eight-year mark, MemorialCare has logged $62 million in savings documented through lean, and it has really become our way of life—truly a management system."

Along the way, MemorialCare system leaders also learned to stop measuring every dollar spent and saved in lean projects.

This is a contentious issue in the majority of lean transformations I have witnessed. Some faction of senior managers usually wants return on investment (ROI) strictly measured. At the beginning of a lean transformation, people see the bill for consulting services and the cost of creating and staffing the central improvement team, and they worry. For the first two and a half years of ThedaCare's lean transformation, I needed to track all money spent on consulting and apply it against any increased revenue or savings from improvement work.

Helen Macfie had the same issue. Leadership did not want to add any additional expenses to the 10-year budget and insisted that Macfie prove that the lean initiative was, at the very least, cost neutral. "In those first three or four years, we spent quite a bit of time—too much time—trying to collect and record the information on all those dollars hiding inside departmental spreadsheets all over the organization," Macfie says. "We would add up the expense of consultants, of taking people off their regular work to be on the improvement team, and match that up against the redeployed FTEs and the improvements that generated more revenue.

"In year four, I really started to see this wasn't healthy. People were working hard and making huge improvements and then fighting at the end of a project to justify it with dollars," Macfie says.

Macfie and I then essentially did the same thing: set up meetings with our CFOs, showed that lean improvements had sent tens of millions of dollars to the bottom line—even after the costs of consulting, travel, and training—and asked to please stop this wasteful measuring. Fortunately, we both had forward-thinking CFOs, and the ROI calculations for every event ceased.

I now strongly recommend that organizations resist the urge to measure ROI from the beginning. Not only is it wasteful but also it signals to people that lean is a cost-savings initiative, which is absolutely wrong. Lean is a cultural transformation. It does not work unless quality, staff morale, and cost improve together. To have people measure ROI for every improvement project overly emphasizes the cost part of the equation.

Once a year now, Macfie is asked for the improvement system numbers for the annual report. Using a simpler accounting that does not mine the minutiae of every event, she can say that after eight years, their lean improvement work has sent $62 million to MemorialCare's bottom line. Still, if it were up to her, we would be talking about something else entirely: lives saved, better service in the EDs, happier staff.

If you do need to show ROI, make sure that you equally emphasize the other critical metrics. While planning and building the model cell, come to agreement on what will be measured and how in order to reflect the truth of changes to quality, staff morale, and cost. Cost is important, but it is only one aspect of lean.

Because every lean transformation will take on a different form, let's now go to HealthEast in St. Paul, Minnesota and see the Inside Expert approach to building a central improvement team.

As the new CEO, and formerly the president of hospitals at ThedaCare during its transformation, Kathryn Correia arrived in Minnesota in 2012 knowing that she would build a lean infrastructure at HealthEast. It was a big job. Kathryn had an entire health system to woo over. As an experienced lean leader, she knew how profound the change to a lean operating system would be. She needed everyone in the same boat.

Early on, Kathryn and a small leadership team met with consulting groups that could provide the Training Wheels approach. In those meetings, however, she knew she was hearing consultants describe a more tools-only approach instead of a system-wide cultural transformation. Another consulting group, one with a system-wide approach, seemed too brash for HealthEast. Physicians and leaders with HealthEast had a long history of taking pride in their quality scores while downplaying some serious financial hurdles, and Kathryn knew that criticism from outsiders could create distrust.

So, Kathryn and her team kept looking and stumbled on the road less taken, which might be called Inside Expert. Here, you hire one very experienced lean leader to lead and train the central improvement team and to coordinate all improvement efforts from the inside. I do not recommend this path unless the CEO has some depth of experience with lean and knows what questions to ask of a potential Inside Expert. As Kathryn, my friend and former ThedaCare colleague, will confirm, the leader has to know what she does not know before taking this path.

As president of the ThedaCare hospitals division, Kathryn had been immersed in lean for eight years before she was lured to neighboring Minnesota to become CEO of HealthEast. With four hospitals, multiple clinics, and about $1 billion in annual revenue, HealthEast is comparable in size to ThedaCare. Kathryn knew the health system needed lean thinking, but she was also sensitive to being the new leader in an established system with its own culture.

"Coming to a new place is like going on that cooking show *Chopped*, where you get a basket of really different ingredients and you have to make something of it," Kathryn says. "The trick is to highlight the best ingredient you've got."

Being a lean thinker, Kathryn chose to highlight a couple of big improvement projects. But she also recognized that these projects were completed largely with heroic actions outside normal ways of doing things. What she wanted was a culture of steady, sustainable continuous improvement throughout the organization.

"We needed a central improvement office. I knew it wasn't my job to build this office, but I needed the skill set to stay close with me," she says.

Quickly, Kathryn identified two change leaders in the organization: Cara Hull, an engineer, and Julie Schmidt, the chief administrative officer who was close to retirement but still strongly interested in improvement. Together, they took a senior team on a few field trips to see what good looked like. One day, they found themselves at Andersen Windows, where Cara Hull had contacts.

"And here we got lucky because we got to walk around with [plant manager] Didier Rabino, watching him walk through his morning management work. Now, I had been working with the daily management system at ThedaCare before I left, so I knew what he was doing, but I was watching his version," Kathryn says. "We saw how information flowed from the front line to the area coordinator up to Didier, and it was elegant. The escalation process [of problems] was transparent. Everything was just powerful yet understated."

Equally as important, Kathryn said, the environment was respectful. While they were watching, an employee had a problem picking material from a bin. The worker stopped the line, and an area coordinator and manager came to the area and, as a group, used PDSA thinking to come up with a corrective action plan. Nobody was afraid to talk about problems. "You can't fake that stuff," Kathryn says. "This was the culture we wanted."

Driving back home from the plant, Kathryn said, "Wouldn't it be nice to have a consultant like Didier?" Schmidt replied, "Why don't we ask him?"

While Rabino had no background in healthcare, Kathryn saw a leader who would pay attention to the culture and to every detail of a process and who created an atmosphere of respect. It is a unique combination of skills and personality.

Having one sensei create a central improvement office and launch a lean operating system is full of hazards. Kathryn knew to avoid mistakes such as bombarding the organization with unconnected rapid-improvement events or allowing people to become complacent after snacking on low-hanging fruit. So she listened carefully as Rabino described the journey that he believed an organization should make. Knowing that a cultural transformation was her real aim, Kathryn was intrigued with Rabino's plans to begin change both bottom up and top down.

Rather than beginning lean work with rapid-improvement events at the front line, Rabino began with aspects of a daily improvement system—involving managers and staff in addressing problems with PDSA thinking—and with strategy deployment at the executive level.

"Within nine months, everyone had a visual management board, and leaders were conducting daily huddles. They were using PDSA and idea cards for improvement," Kathryn says. "Didier's approach was to go broad with everyone learning PDSA thinking. Only now [two years later] do we have a model cell.

"At the same time, he had us starting strategy deployment. We meet once a week now around strategy deployment, and Didier coaches us, but he also has facilitators rotate through the position in our meetings so everyone knows strategy deployment."

Some of Rabino's ideas were unusual, but Kathryn was willing to take a chance. After all, this was Rabino's third time introducing a lean system to an organization. A former cabinetmaker turned engineer and production manager, Rabino studied with many lean masters while at Steelcase in England and France before moving to the United States.

Beginning in 1999, Rabino worked with David Mann[42] to create a lean system at Steelcase in Michigan. In 2004, Rabino moved to building the lean system at Andersen Windows, including daily management systems, company-wide training, and strong central improvement offices. Both Steelcase and Andersen Windows became widely known for their robust lean cultures.

When it came time to create the central improvement office that Rabino would lead at HealthEast, he wanted to keep it very small— much smaller than the 1% of FTEs that Kathryn was expecting.

"We do not want a *do-it-for-me* model," Rabino explains with the French accent of his native land. "This is disrespectful, because it takes away opportunities for a leader to learn.

"If I keep my capacity [in the lean office] small, when a leader calls me up and asks for someone who will do a project for him, I can say, 'No, I can't do that.' Then, I can teach this leader how to do his own project. If I do it for him, we would have short-term results but deny that leader the chance to become a better leader."

Rabino's argument is certainly interesting and, in the end, he and Kathryn settled on a hybrid model, keeping fewer than 10 facilitators on the improvement team but moving them through—and up through—the

---

42. Author of *Creating a Lean Culture* (CRC Press: 2010)

organization fairly quickly. Rabino expects to train more facilitators who will stay embedded in their own areas. Meanwhile, he is focused on giving intensive workshops in skill development such as leading projects with A3.

With such a small central improvement office, Rabino has been very careful about whom he selects for these critical roles, and he has some advice. "When I look at résumés, my red flags are ISO 9000 and Six Sigma, because ISO is focused on compliance not improvement and Six Sigma trains people to work alone for long stretches of time, instead of developing people. This does not mean that these people are bad, only that they might need to relearn. Lean requires people who are curious, driven by the need to learn. We need teachers and coaches who are capable of discipline and resilience and, most of all, who have the capacity to listen. Humility is not on the résumé, but that is what we need."

Taking the Inside Expert path is less common in healthcare, but HealthEast is seeing results comparable to those taking the Training Wheels approach. Along with a greater emphasis on standard work and scientific thinking, the revenue/cost margin at this nonprofit system has never been higher. Historically below 2% and usually less, the margin has risen to 3%. Patient satisfaction scores are steadily rising, and an EPIC implementation, using lots of employee-generated idea cards and PDSA thinking in the preparatory stages, went far smoother than such things usually go. In 2014, HealthEast was proudly counting 29,400 improvement ideas implemented—meaning checked and verified—in a year.

"My one concern at the beginning was that Didier would leave before we were up and running," Kathryn says. "That didn't happen, and now I see that this rollout was absolutely the right decision for this organization."

At three organizations taking different paths to lean deployment, MemorialCare, ThedaCare, and HealthEast, we have seen three manifestations of the central improvement team with some very important commonalities that illustrate the essential framework. A central improvement team needs a dedicated full-time staff, with either a solid or dotted reporting line to the CEO, and must be used as a pipeline for developing future leaders. The central improvement team, where everyone receives and eventually spreads lean training, is the keeper of the flame. The other details, such as how many people are in the office and whether you select a Training Wheels or an Inside Expert approach, must be dictated by individual circumstances.

At HealthEast, the top-down, bottom-up plan worked in large part due to Rabino's reliance on a daily management system including huddle boards, visual management, and standard work for leaders. This was also critical in the lean deployment at ThedaCare and MemorialCare, too. So, it is time that we introduce the line management method work that becomes the central nervous system of a lean organization.

5

The Daily
Management System

The young man in the middle of the room was absolutely still except for his chest, which rose and fell in shudders, in time with the ventilator. The room was tiny and filled with the coppery smell of blood and medicines, but the ICU nurse did not seem to notice as she flew through her tasks. She went up on tiptoe, leaned over the young man, and stretched past the bed's headboard to reach the oxygen controls. Then she bent nearly double to reach through a small forest of IV poles and controls before she found the right one to adjust. Deftly she moved through every obstacle in her way, as she seemed to focus on nothing but this young trauma patient and his tenuous grasp on life.

In the corner of the room, the young man's family clutched each other and tried not to sob too loudly. They were so respectful of the nurse's work that I felt even worse. In that tiny room where their son and brother was likely dying, we did not even have chairs on which they could sit.

Outside of the room, I walked quickly through the corridors of Theda Clark Hospital; I was afraid to stop and talk to anyone for fear the tight band of anger around my chest would break. And then I realized that this was exactly why I was going to gemba: I had seen real problems in that ICU room, and, as CEO, I was just the person to start working on solutions.

In my office, I called Kathryn Correia, then president of ThedaCare's hospitals division, and blurted, "The ICU rooms are a mess. The ergonomics for the nurses are terrible. Someone is going to get hurt, and there was no place for that poor family to sit."

Kathryn sighed and said, "I know. We need to redesign that whole area."

"We have a bond project going to the board for approval," I reminded her.

"Yes, but the cap was $91 million, and the ICU project didn't fit," she said.

This was 2008. In another building, a vice president of the hospitals division named Kim Barnas was already working with a team to create a daily management system that made sense for the lean organization we were creating. We were not there yet, but this case demonstrates both the need for such a system and its power.

Every chief executive who has spent time at gemba truly watching operations with open eyes has been in my position. As I walked away from that hospital room, I was angry but also filled with dismay. I had read all the reports about our great quality statistics. I had participated on teams correcting situations like that ergonomic nightmare in the ICU. I thought we were better than this. Everyone around me was always anxious to deliver good news when what I really needed was all the bad news.

Meanwhile, frontline caregivers such as that ICU nurse were straining their bodies and apologizing to patients' families and *not complaining*. I could see it in the practiced way the nurse stretched for the oxygen controls on tiptoes. She did that every day, and that's just the way it was.

We needed what every organization needs: a constructive pipeline for intelligence from the front line that flows up through the organization and an equally robust line of communication and strategy from the top back to the front line. In the book that Kim Barnas would write on creating a lean management system,[43] she described it as an atmospheric system, where facts on the ground rise like vapor from a lake to mix with the decisions and strategies that fall from above. In the cloud, strategies are informed by facts on the ground, and decisions made at the top are relevant to the front line.

The daily management system is now defined as standardized work at all levels of management to enable a daily dialogue about the most important facts of the business. It is designed to ensure that everyone is working on the right problems.

It requires thoughtful action and discipline in order to collect daily intelligence from the front line, test and implement improvement ideas, and keep strategies relevant. Kim's book describes this system in detail, so here I will cover only the essential pieces of standard work for each management level, with a description of how each level fits into the other.

The senior leadership team, generally referred to as the C-suite, is responsible for setting the True North metrics that will guide the organization and indicate whether you are winning or losing. Leaders also establish the targets for True North performance, stating how they

---

43. Kim Barnas, *Beyond Heroes: A Lean Management System for Healthcare* (ThedaCare Center for Healthcare Value: 2014)

expect to improve the existing True North metric over the next year. From that discussion, leaders dive into strategy deployment by looking at the critical few key initiatives that are aimed at achieving the goals tied to True North. At ThedaCare, we worked hard to winnow strategic initiatives to fewer than three per year. These are major efforts that take up a lot of system resources, such as employee safety, and so must be limited in number. Senior management standard work also includes participating in regular gemba walks, using visual management, and learning and teaching A3 thinking.

Standard work for vice presidents and division heads also includes regular gemba walks, visual management, A3 thinking, as well as regular auditing of team huddles, mentoring and coaching future leaders, and working on strategic initiatives.

Managers' standard work includes daily meetings, or huddles, with supervisors, lead-shift nurses, and team members in front of a visual management board documenting all continuous-improvement work to talk through needs, discuss progress on improvement projects, and consider new ideas. Every current continuous-improvement project is on one of these boards, with progress being tracked by the unit. Directors and vice presidents routinely attend these team huddles to observe, mentor, and find barriers they might be able to knock down. Managers, vice presidents, and the president of the hospitals also routinely audit standard work to look for deviations and to verify that the standard, as written, still describes the best way to do the work.

Supervisors or managers meet with lead-shift nurses at the beginning of every shift to talk through preset questions such as, "Who might be a fall risk on your unit today?" and "Are there any staffing issues?" After this status meeting, supervisors meet with their manager (one step higher on the ThedaCare organizational chart), to go through slightly broader questions that align with strategic and local initiatives.

Similar conversations occur between senior executives on a weekly basis. All of these conversations help identify continuous-improvement opportunities.

Kim and her team helped ensure that everyone had time for these huddles, status checks, and gemba walks by declaring that every weekday morning between 8 and 10 a.m. is a no-meeting zone. During this time, all managers are focused on the needs of the frontline caregivers and on improving patient care instead of being locked away in department meetings.

The upward-flowing path of information includes an escalation protocol for problems that are judged an immediate threat to safety or quality. ThedaCare's protocol consists of a sentence: If you cannot fix the problem in 15 minutes or less, bring it to your boss. If the boss is not available, people are expected bring the problem to someone else who is one step up. That means that the CEO can be notified of any serious frontline issue within an hour or 90 minutes.

Consider the implications. In most hospitals, the VP or president would not hear of an immediate issue on the floor for 30 days and would then spend an inordinate amount of time simply trying to find out what really happened and whom to blame. With good communication, a focus on process, and a clear escalation protocol, ThedaCare can now fix problems in real time instead of investigating them endlessly but inconclusively or covering them up.

Meanwhile, the executive team establishes the organization's True North and then sets goals for those metrics such as "eliminate preventable mortality" and "zero employee injuries." Working toward these goals requires strategic initiatives, and the really hard work is limiting the number of those initiatives in order to focus everyone's attention. It took ThedaCare years to whittle 33 strategic initiatives down to three, but we kept at it because those 33 initiatives were demanding something like 80% of leaders' attention and leaving just 20% for continuous improvement at the front line.

Since that time, I have advocated a 20/80 rule. Anyone who devotes time and energy to strategic initiatives should do so just 20% of the time and leave the remaining 80% for the important continuous-improvement work at the front line, including rapid-improvement events, value-stream mapping, and standard work auditing. Adopting a rule like this reminds everyone what is most important.

Had this system been in place in 2008, with timely information flowing freely up and down the chain, I would have known that the ICU rooms in Theda Clark Hospital were a safety issue. And while I was creating the $91-million bond issue to bring to the board of trustees, I would have done what I eventually did: expand my request to $95 million based on the recommendations of a cross-functional team led by ICU nurses that redesigned the rooms. At the same time, everyone would have known that I was preparing a bond request focused on creating better patient experiences and the problems in those ICU rooms would have been more urgently brought to my attention.

About two years after Kim and her team put together ThedaCare's daily management system in 2009, it became the star attraction for visitors who came to Appleton to learn about lean in healthcare. Because it was the missing piece in so many lean efforts, we persuaded Kim to teach a course for visitors on how to create a daily management system. In the first year, 240 organizations were represented in those classrooms and the system was being replicated across North America. Still, the question that Kim and I heard repeatedly was and is, "Where do I begin?"

The answer is: begin where you need it most, with the tools that seem most likely to be useful. For example, when Mary Kingston, the new

COO of Providence Little Company of Mary (PLCOM), first arrived at its 450-bed hospital in Los Angeles County, she needed to get to know her executive team. So she began with a daily gemba walk with eight of her direct reports: the directors of the emergency department, surgery, case management, support services, and specialty services such as radiation oncology; the manager of clinical nutrition services; and the directors of the laboratory, blood bank, and pathology.

Then she introduced her colleagues to "morning status conversations" by using a daily set of scripted questions with each person in order to better understand the concerns of her direct reports. While she was getting to know them, Kingston was also coaching her new colleagues in using morning status conversation, which they call trackers, with their direct reports.

Three years into her tenure at PLCOM, Kingston had implemented much of the daily management system in the ICU and ED, including visual management boards and huddles. Other areas of the hospital, meanwhile, were preparing to begin the work.

"The old saying is true: this really is a process," Kingston says. "What I have found is that having daily teaching moments is priceless for moving the culture forward. That's why we, as leaders, need to stay involved and out on the floor. Teaching people to work through a problem by doing it with them is how we change the culture."

When thinking about how to move a visual management board and the practice of daily huddles past the model–cell stage, Kingston realized that she needed to develop leaders who knew not only how to run a huddle but also what they wanted to track on their visual management boards. It was crucial, she said, that they all make those decisions together. So, she began by conducting a leadership huddle around the strategy board.

This is a 30-minute executive meeting held four days a week, in which one leader—a new one each day—presents information and updates everyone on the important initiatives for safety, quality, engagement, or financial stewardship. Senior leaders, including CEO Liz Dunne, take turns presenting as a way to prepare to coach and mentor others who will be conducting the daily huddles.

"Huddles should not be punitive. There needs to be a dialogue, but we also need to be disciplined regarding time and topic," Kingston says. "Everyone is bringing his or her gifts to the huddle. Some people are more disciplined about data; others are better with dialogue. We are learning from each other what works."

Senior leaders are also preparing to launch the two-hour no-meeting zone throughout the hospital. While other organizations have begun their daily management systems with no-meeting zones, Kingston has been cautious of making any unilateral changes. She considers the no-meeting zone vital to the health of a daily management system, but she did not want to force the idea on her team. She needed to lead them to the zone instead of pushing them there.

A system of daily management is a major change for an organization, both in work content and in career trajectory,[44] but I do not believe there is one right way to get started. For example, Jeff Mainland, executive vice president of SickKids in Ontario, Canada, launched the hospital's new management efforts with two model cells of the daily management system. On the neurosurgery unit and a general medicine unit, they implemented every module of the system that Kim outlined in her book. Once it was running smoothly and other managers were asking to get trained on this system that seemed to make

---

44. Career trajectories change because a daily management system rewards a different style of leadership. Instead of bold, shoot-from-the-hip charisma, lean leaders are valued for teaching, mentoring, and using the scientific method to address issues and benefit patients.

everyone's life easier, Mainland and his team rolled out the changes to all units.

By contrast, Mike Conroy, chief medical officer at Palo Alto Medical Foundation, chose to take pieces of the management system and incorporate them into the working structure of the first model cell they created at the Fremont, California, clinic. So, from the very beginning, physicians, nurses, and medical assistants all learned that daily status conversations and huddle boards were part of their lean systems.

For every leader considering how and whether to go through the hard work of creating a daily management system, the questions to ask are: Do I have access to accurate information from the front line? Will I know when something happens that needs my attention? If the answer is no, you need to act decisively.

Most organizations do not have a real management system at all. Leaders are used to intuiting problems and then telling others how to fix everything. And while it is true that intuition is quicker and less cumbersome than collecting data, creating communication systems, and visiting gemba, it is inaccurate much of the time. One of the most difficult challenges for leaders in every organization is learning how to stop interrupting people with the answer.

To begin creating a daily management system that works for your organization, go to gemba, but do not go alone. Alone, you will find it too easy to fall into old comfortable routines: telling people what to do, offering spontaneous lectures, asking questions such as "Who caused that problem?" Instead, find a coach who can assist you in becoming a respectful, open-minded presence at gemba, one who leads with questions instead of answers. Leaders need to unlearn questions such as "Why is the oxygen tank behind the bed?" or even "Is that oxygen tank in the best place for you?" Both of these questions presume the answer and may imply that the nurse should have already identified and fixed the issue.

Think of how you would respond, if you were that nurse, to instead being asked "Is that oxygen tank in the best place for you?" or "How would you suggest we position that tank?" On the gemba, leaders need to phrase questions very carefully to make sure that they are seen as helpful instead of judgmental.

The coach who helps senior leaders unlearn bad behaviors at gemba should know the Socratic method of posing questions and be trusted enough to feel comfortable offering very personal feedback. A good coach will be able to tell the CEO when he or she is backsliding. But a coach is not the only solution.

There are many good books on how to ask open-ended, Socratic questions.[45] A book is a good place to start, although most of us will still need a good bit of monitoring and reminding to keep from backsliding into dogmatism. I recommend that all senior leaders receive some training in how to form nonjudgmental questions and then assist each other in creating a respectful, open-minded atmosphere at gemba. It is a less expensive option than hiring personal coaches for the entire staff.

All of this is going to be crucial for the next phase of your lean transformation: spreading the work of the model cell to all parts of the organization. Without spread, you will have a lonely island of excellence, doomed to extinction. That is not the goal for any lean transformation. So, let us turn to the whole organization.

---

45. A good place to begin is "Leading with Questions" by Michael Marquardt.

6

Spreading
the Work

By the time you are ready to spread the work of the model cell to beta sites and then to the rest of your organization, much will have changed.

The model cell should be your star attraction, an enviable island of excellence that has received so much attention and resource that it may provoke jealousy. The central improvement office will be staffed with newly trained lean facilitators. Frontline caregivers and managers will be meeting every day for huddles and status conferences, moving problems and ideas for improvement up the line while aligning projects with organizational strategies proposed at the top and confirmed with feedback from the bottom.

If you have done it right, you will feel a palpable anticipation—even tension—in the hallways and conference rooms at this point. This is called *pull*. Think of it as someone tugging on your sleeve and asking for some of that. People on the outside of the model cell looking in will want to borrow the tools, get the extra training, and dive in right now.

Even those who are nervous about change would rather have it over with. After all, they have seen how serious the effort is, and they keep hearing that this is the organization's future. Even people who are change resistant can find waiting to be excruciating. This is not the time, however, to be hasty.

The model cell is a complex machine. More than processes have changed here; people have questioned their habits, adjusted their thinking, and changed how they think of work. Those early-adopter physicians, nurses, assistants, and administrators who built and run the model cell have come to new attitudes—often after some hard slogging. This is why the model cell works and also why it cannot be simply picked up and plopped down on any unit or clinic in the organization.

Creating pull, the desire among employees to try continuous improvement, is step one, and it is essential. The next step requires a critical decision. Should your organization select one or two beta sites and begin training the people who work there to replicate the original model cell in their site? Or should you break down all of the necessary skills and concepts into instructional modules and teach the model cell in increments to the whole organization?

The replication model allows people to learn by doing. This is good. Modular learning enables an entire organization to learn concepts together. This is also good. The deciding factor is the circumstances of your organization and culture. Your needs must dictate the methods.

Fortunately, one lean leader has used both methods in quick succession and learned some valuable lessons. James Hereford is now the chief operating officer of Stanford University Hospital and Clinics. In 2009 he was in a similar position at the integrated care system Group Health in Seattle, followed by a position as COO at Palo Alto Medical

Foundation (PAMF), which was introduced earlier. In short, James has led some very large and exciting lean healthcare transformations.

Group Health and PAMF each have about 1,000 physicians working over more than two dozen sites. For each organization, James used model cells to introduce lean thinking at busy outpatient clinics. But this is where the paths diverge.

Group Health is a member-governed nonprofit healthcare and insurance system that serves about 600,000 people in Washington State. One of the early and enthusiastic adopters of lean thinking, James and Group Health had few organizations to emulate when it came time to spread the work of the model cell across the organization. But most of us can think back to school and figure out how to teach a complicated subject. Educators break down the material into digestible chunks and teach it to everyone.

James and Michael Erikson, who was vice president of primary care at the time, looked at the Group Health model cell and found that it contained seven main components that needed to be taught. These were proactively managing care for existing patients through the Internet; chronic disease management; outreach for patients with unmet medical needs; previsit standard work; postvisit summaries; standard work for the daily huddle; and call management to try to resolve issues with the patient's first telephone call.

Frontline teams created training materials for each component, prepared to teach each module across the organization, and leaders such as James and Michael went out to spread the good news to the clinics. Here was where they stumbled.

"The problem was we did a tell-and-sell. We went into each clinic and described the model cell and all the benefits they would be getting, and I think the natural human reaction to that is resistance," James says.

"So, we heard a lot of reasons why our processes wouldn't work in that clinic. 'We're different,' people said, or, 'My patients are different.'

"The real problem was that we didn't ask; we told."

At gemba, during multiple visits to the clinics where change was supposed to be happening, Michael Erikson heard the loud drumbeat of displeasure at the front line.

"I had quite a few hard conversations with physicians and frontline leaders. They said we were being disingenuous about how the work was going to be improved. We had told them they would be shaping the changes. Then we showed up with a package to sell," Michael says. "There's only so many conversations like that you can have before you realize you need to change the way you're leading."

The leadership team regrouped and then went back to the clinics with their curriculum and one important change. At every site, they taught clinic staff how to do PDSA on each core element of the curriculum in order to customize and create ownership of the material. As frontline teams began creating iterative improvements to the original curriculum—and to their workflow—confidence grew. Employee engagement scores dramatically improved, according to surveys conducted by an industry-standard external survey service.

It is not always easy going to gemba. It leaves one open to getting buttonholed and having occasionally unpleasant conversations. But if Michael had not been there, he would not have known why the work was going awry.

"Leadership is about learning and always being willing to change, based on what you learn," Michael says.

Meanwhile, James went to his next position thinking about how to reduce resistance from the outset.

Oct → Feb

Exam

Error Proof Systems

Six processes 1st, people last.

★ 1:1 staff engagement

Acknowledge vs Success story

"The Nudge" "Beyond Ideas"

Eight hundred miles south, in Palo Alto, California, where James became COO of PAMF in 2011, he joined Dr. Susan Knox, a regional medical director; Dr. Rupal Badani, a pediatrician leader; and others to put together that model cell in the Fremont clinic described in chapter 1. While they were working with teams to design new workflows, they were also talking about how people approach a new idea. They want to "kick the tires," James says. They want to put their hands on it and understand how the various pieces interact.

Learning a new idea in modules is a bit like getting your first car piece by piece in the mail, he decided. Even with clear instructions about how to put it together, you lack crucial information about how the different components support the work of the others. Also, you do not know how to drive.

So, James and Dr. Michael Conroy, introduced in the previous chapter, opted for beta-site whole-clinic implementations—with the model cell's new systems now spread throughout an entire clinic—thus providing greater transparency from the beginning. During the design phase of the Fremont clinic model cell, they invited clinical and administrative leaders from throughout the organization to join the team and help create the future system. After it was up and running, they invited leaders from throughout the other 26 sites to come and kick the tires.

Then the PAMF leadership team chose three beta sites. Each beta site was selected for leaders who were very open to trying a new system and who each had a compelling reason to abandon their old ways. They were ripe for change.

At each beta site, they gathered the leaders and helped them create a current-state value-stream map of their clinic. James and his team then described the results being achieved at the Fremont clinic. James said,

"Here is our best thinking to date on how to make a better clinic. Does it make sense for you?"

They talked through each clinic's unique needs and whether they should adopt the various components of the model clinic—including simplifying and standardizing the supply chain, new call-management systems, better patient flow, and new methods for managing physician in-baskets—or adapt the work to fit the clinic's individual needs.

The toughest aspect of the new system for physicians to accept was giving up their private offices in order to sit with their medical assistants in an open area. In Fremont, this co-location had been proven to foster better daily communication, help to improve patient flow in the clinic, and decrease errors and rework. In the model cell, it worked great. But reaction to the idea of co-location varied wildly.

One pediatrician stood up at the end of a training session that dealt with patient flow and co-location and said, "This is what is going to stop me from retiring."

Others were aghast. A doctor without a private office? It seemed like a clear loss of status. Where would they put their old textbooks?

In the end, lean leaders realized they needed to change the way they talked about co-location. On the insistence of one physician, they renamed it MA–MD Synchronization. Instead of dwelling on the loss of an office, they emphasized the fact that, with less miscommunication and rework, physicians were closing files and finishing their workdays much earlier. And then James issued a challenge.

"We showed them the model-cell processes and challenged them to meet it or beat it," James says. "If they thought they had a better way to achieve the results—less waiting time for patients, better quality, etc.— and could convince their peer beta sites that it was a worthy experiment, then we would help them run it. And we did a couple of those. But 95% of the time, they ended up adopting what we had done at Fremont because it worked."

Physicians were also primed to adopt the Fremont work by doctor testimonials. Out of the 55 family practitioners at Fremont, five or six became ambassadors for the lean transformation, Dr. Conroy says. The physician ambassadors gave tours of Fremont and were videotaped discussing the new patient flow through the clinics. Those videos were then shown at town hall meetings at the other clinics. Doctors listen to other doctors.

As they began training people in the beta clinics, lean leaders developed working theories about whom to train and how to train them. In every clinic, they met people who were excited to change the system, some who were cautious, and a few who were deeply reluctant, Dr. Conroy says. The last group, while small, could be very vocal, demanding to see proof of the new method's effectiveness with hard data and throwing up roadblocks whenever possible.

Lean facilitators found that if they offered training to the most willing participants first, those people returned to their jobs energized for the new way. The middle majority—those who were merely cautious—saw that energy and were more inclined to be open to change and seek out training.

"We deliberately left the skeptics until the end," says Dr. Conroy, who took over more responsibility for the spread of lean thinking after James left for Stanford. "So, they watched the changes taking place for several weeks. They knew what was going to happen and, finally, they had to get on board or be left behind."

It took about 18 months to spread the work of the model cell to all of PAMF's primary care clinics. In that time, every physician gave up his or her office in order to sit with a medical assistant. (Although, one deeply resistant doctor did outline his area with large potted plants to preserve at least the idea of private space.)

Close to two years after the primary care conversion, when James Hereford had left for Stanford and Michael Erikson had joined PAMF as COO, Dr. Conroy, Michael, and the lean team prepared to bring lean thinking into the specialty clinics. Their first stop was gastroenterology, and "the first thing those doctors said was, 'We're not primary care. There's no way that system will work here,'" Dr. Conroy says, smiling.

During that meeting, Michael recalls asking the change-resistant physicians for their biggest problems about work. The answer: lack of access to the endoscopy suite. Physicians often had difficulty getting time for their patients in that ambulatory surgery center. So, Michael and Dr. Conroy and their teams began there. They used 5S to organize and standardize the OR rooms. They had endoscopy team members join them in redesigning workflows for every team member and, very quickly, increased capacity in the endoscopy suite by 30%.

"This is what got the doctors' attention," Michael says. "Now, we could move to their office-based workflows and determine how to adopt what had been learned in primary care."

Of course, that does not mean adoption was simple. Once again, physicians balked at the idea of giving up their offices and had a hard time visualizing their practices operating using the new workflow methods in primary care. PAMF arranged field trips for the gastroenterologists to see what lean practices looked like in other organizations far beyond PAMF. At Park Nicollet Health Services near Minneapolis, one PAMF physician approached a host doctor and said, "I don't see that you have co-located or given up your offices."

The other physician shook his head. Co-location had never been part of Park Nicollet's lean efforts, he said, and what's more, he did not think he would like it very much. That story was retold often among PAMF doctors for a while as proof that co-location was not necessary.

What happened next is not uncommon. The PAMF physician who came back from Park Nicollet kept working through the transition and investigating new methods while looking for evidence that lean did not work. What he found in the way of evidence from the PAMF experiments surprised him enough that he changed his views and became a real supporter of the lean work, even making videos to introduce the new workflow to his fellow gastroenterologists.

As Dr. Conroy, Michael, and leaders at other health systems have discovered, there is friction at the heart of spreading this work, and that friction is unavoidable because the two key principles at play here are standardization and customization. The model cell must be standardized in order to be replicated, yet needs of individual clinics and units demand that the model cell is tailored to local needs.

At ThedaCare, thinking on how to do this evolved over time. When we opened our first Collaborative Care unit, an inpatient general medicine unit, leaders first asked for nurses, hospitalists, pharmacists, physical therapists, and case managers to apply for positions on the breakthrough unit. Then the new system's designers broke the concepts into modules and created teaching materials.

"We had new care plans, new ways of doing documentation," says Shana Herzfeldt, RN, who was on the original Collaborative Care design team and is now director of clinical operations for ThedaCare's two largest hospitals. "There was a lot of change. So, we took nurses offline for six weeks, training them to the model.

"When we went to our second unit, we took everyone offline for two or three weeks. After that, I'm not sure if we took a whole week because it wasn't always feasible to take an entire unit offline for training. So, we focused more on job shadowing."

Another training method they used was a "switch-up," putting a couple of nurses from an experienced Collaborative Care unit into a unit that was about to transform, in exchange for nurses from the new unit who needed to experience the Collaborative Care way.

Even before anyone received training, however, leaders from Collaborative Care and the organizational development department began each unit's transformation with a cultural assessment. That might sound like something New Age and ethereal, but it is entirely practical. For instance, the Collaborative Care model relied on licensed practical nurses to perform certain tasks so that registered nurses could devote themselves to other functions. Finding out whether people on the unit were comfortable working with LPNs and whether there was resistance to such an idea was important to know up front and helped guide the training.

Similarly in our outpatient clinics, the new model required medical assistants to draw blood for testing in the in-clinic laboratory. This was a critical piece of the puzzle that allowed us to provide fresh lab results within about 15 minutes, delivered to the patient's EMR during the exam. Having MAs draw blood required new training, but technique was not the only issue. Some of our most valued assistants were unsure about performing any kind of invasive procedure. One or two were downright squeamish. This had never been what they expected to do, and a few were very uncomfortable. It was critical work to uncover these issues, calmly and productively, and then find ways to move these valued assistants into their new roles.

When the Collaborative Care model spread past the inpatient medicine units, leaders had to be even more flexible, Shana says. One of the most crucial pieces of standard work on the general medicine units, for instance, was the bedside care conference between patient, physician, nurse, case manager, social worker, pharmacist, and family members within 90 minutes of admission. This one change in workflow had radically moved quality and satisfaction numbers. But would it make sense on a surgical unit?

"Our bedside care conferences look very different for a medical-unit patient with several comorbidities than it will for a patient on a surgical unit, when the surgery has been planned for weeks. That first care conference might take 45 minutes on a medical unit. But when it came to a surgery that had been well planned far in advance, a lot of the assessments have already been done. So, we had a hard time getting surgeons to go on rounds with the nurse," Shana says. "In those cases, we finally arrived at an agreement that, at the minimum, the surgeon would pick up a telephone and call the nurse within 90 minutes of admission."

More importantly, surgeons—most of whom are independent and not employed by ThedaCare—became more actively engaged in the new system once they understood that leadership was listening to them and were prepared to change standards that did not work for their practices. This is the third principle of a successful spread, along with customization and standardization: fingerprints. The caregivers of every clinic and unit that adopts the new work of the model cell must feel that their fingerprints are all over the work.

When this kind of customization is encouraged, innovative new ideas often emerge. For instance, orthopedic surgical units pointed out that their care plans did not begin in the hospital. Surgeries were usually planned weeks ahead, and every case included prework and postoperative care. So, lean leaders attached an RN case manager to follow these patients from the clinic to the hospital and home again. That continuity of care helped reduce defects, rework, and miscommunication.

The experiment also managed to eliminate the standardized presurgery classes that patients were attending—that were too often not relevant for the patient—in favor of one-on-one learning with the RN case manager.

"What we have found is that spread never ends," Shana says. "Even if we have all the units working on our new model of care, someone comes up with a great idea, and then we're working on spreading that."

Because spread never ends, it is helpful to formalize the process with the three main pillars in mind: standardization, customization, and fingerprints.

For the spread of a model cell to ThedaCare's outpatient clinics, for instance, leaders always began with a cultural assessment, a two-day retreat, and a customized master plan—complete with tollgates and benchmarks—created by the lean facilitator and clinic leaders.

Kathleen Franklin, an internal consultant for ThedaCare's organizational development department, remembers navigating the early spread of new work in outpatient clinics with the help of a compact with physicians. Not a contract. A contract sounds like lawyers would be involved. A compact, Kathy says, allowed leaders to lay out the framework of the change that was proposed without being autocratic.

The compact might say that administrators would not make any personnel decisions that affected physicians without talking to them in advance. It might also state that the clinic would be expected to get same-day lab results for patients, create a standard method for assistants to settling patients in a room, and have all assistants trained in phlebotomy. Then the clinic leaders, lean facilitators, and Kathy or another internal consultant from organizational development would work out the detailed plan from there. This allowed for everyone's fingerprints to be on the plan customized for that clinic, which also adhered to the standards that all clinics were adopting.

What is important is that leaders were not handing standard work to the staff in these clinics and saying, "Do this." People are entirely resistant to being told how to do their work. Instead, Kathy and her team tried to offer a set of goalposts, a few rules of the game, and some best practices of teams that had scored before and encouraged the new clinic team to find their own way to the goal.

ThedaCare's methods were not unlike the adopt-or-adapt methods of Dr. Conroy and Michael Erikson at PAMF. None of us did this perfectly. And not every employee was capable of making the change. However, we kept working at it, changing our methods when we encountered problems and listening to our people tell us what worked and what did not.

"If I could give one bit of advice, it would be this: have patience," Kathy says. "Especially, have patience with the first third of your clinics or units to transform after the model cell. Once you get a critical mass on board, there will be more peer-to-peer resources and learning opportunities. Before that, expect to be flexible and have a lot of conversations about what's important here."

Human beings are often caught in a conundrum. We fear change even while we long to evolve. We want to know the next big thing and ride the wave of the new, yet we protect the status quo.

So, what is the best way to offer our people a sense of safety and familiarity, even while pushing whole-organization transformations? Let's move on in part II to people development, which in many ways is the reason we have come all this way.

Part II

Partners
in the Transformation

7

Developing People

I n 2006, ThedaCare's world was flat. The same was true for a lot of companies following the 1990s flat-management craze. Perhaps you remember it. We were all supposed to foster better communication and faster decision making by cutting out the middle.

My predecessor as CEO spent a lot of time and money with consultants to trim our organizational layers. And, on the face of things, it was a success. We had effectively eliminated the position of supervisor by the early 2000s. Soon thereafter, every manager—one rung above supervisor on the old org chart—was responsible for about 140 staff members. It could take an entire year just to write that many performance reviews, never mind actually getting to know your people.

We did not know why this was wrong, however, until that year, 2006, when I hired a new chief operating officer from the lean manufacturing world. From him we learned that, at its heart, lean is very simply a system for developing people. To do this, managers need time to be mentors. That may sound like a simple need, but moving toward that goal uncovered a cascade of issues, including the way that we performed annual reviews, hired and recruited, and thought about job requirements.

In the end, we discovered that leaders in operations need to partner with people in human resources, education, and organizational development. We needed to bust down our corporate silos in order to truly address the needs of the frontline worker.

It was a hard lesson, but we were fortunate to have a very determined teacher in Matt Furlan, our new COO. Matt had been trained as an industrial engineer and was vice president of operations at the HON Company, a lean forerunner, before he came to ThedaCare. Matt was recommended to me through our sensei, George Koenigsaecker, former president of the HON Company.[46] At the time, ThedaCare had some islands of excellence, but I was determined that we become a truly lean organization. Matt, meanwhile, was not entirely sure how lean might translate into a hospital. But he was willing to try for a personal reason, which I will let him tell.

"My father had been very ill for a long time when George Koenigsaecker told me about ThedaCare," Matt says. "For 18 months, Dad bounced in and out of hospitals and convalescent homes with COPD[47] and dementia. My mother, who had been a nurse for 35 years, hardly ever left his side. She spent all her time trying to make sure he got the right care, and, still, mistakes were made. The worst part, for me, was seeing my mom's terrible guilt at not being able to manage Dad's care. She aged 10 years during that time."

---

46. Koenigsaecker led the 1990s lean conversion of the HON Company, a $1.5-billion office furniture manufacturer. Under his leadership, the organization's volume tripled and it was named by *Industry Week* magazine as one of the "World's Best Managed Companies."

47. Chronic obstructive pulmonary disease.

So, Matt came to us not just as COO but also as a son determined to help create better care for families like his. He spent the first six months or so at ThedaCare shadowing people and learning our strengths and weaknesses. What he saw, he told me later, were managers chasing directives. He saw exhausted people with no capacity beyond working those directives for anything except responding to emergencies (firefighting). Sometimes, staff and managers might get a week off to go to a rapid-improvement event, Matt says. They would learn a lot and then return to their units for more directives, more firefighting. How we were treating our managers was clearly disrespectful.

Finally, Matt was ready to make his recommendations, and Kathryn Correia, our president of the hospitals, told me that Matt was thinking about a very big change. We set up a meeting, and I asked her to bring supporting data for whatever it was they had in mind. I tried to prepare myself. But when Matt told me that we needed to hire back all those supervisors in order to push down the management-staff ratio to 5-1, I was aghast. He wanted us to spend about $1.8 million to bring back the supervisory positions we had just worked years to eliminate?

Matt nodded. Lean required that every frontline worker become a problem solver. But people could not just intuit solutions. They needed to learn how to solve problems methodically, relying only on facts. They needed to reflexively use tools such as PDSA and A3 the way they used pens and telephones, Matt said. Doing this required supervisors who could teach and mentor, and there was no room for either role in our current organizational chart. Money to support the new positions would come from continuous improvement and waste removal, he said. I told him I would think about it.

Nobody likes backpedaling. It had not been my decision to get rid of all our supervisors, but I had supported our previous CEO. I certainly did not want to return to the old days, in which supervisors were too often treated as a manager's lackey, running after low-priority tasks. If we re-created the role, would we seem wishy-washy? I heard what Matt was saying about hardwiring mentors into our organizational chart, but I kept hoping there was some other way. I did not sleep much over the next week.

During this time, we were spreading the work of our Collaborative Care model cell, and I stopped by a new unit one day to observe the work. These units had their own staffing structure, created by nurses as part of the original design. Looking at a chart, I saw that all the nurses were members of small cells. For every five staff members, there was an RN lead, an experienced nurse who was capable of doing all the tasks and acted as a coach and mentor. The lead trained others in standard work, moved into the various roles to teach new skills, and helped her team spot improvement opportunities and work through PDSA problem solving. The lead's role was to help nurses develop their skills. For every five leads, there was a nursing supervisor to teach and mentor the leads in problem solving and skill development.

Our nurses had nearly re-created the Toyota Production System team structure, the same one that Matt was asking us to implement. Watching those teams, I could see that the small-group leader idea was not an outsider's idea; it came from our own frontline intelligence. It was the structure our nurses had chosen for themselves during months of testing and trial runs. How could I say no?

Still, I told Matt and Kathryn that we needed to start small and measure. If we were going to backpedal, we were going to do it with intention and measurable outcomes. They selected two trial units and captured baseline data for staff engagement and delivery on departmental measures. Then we set up a system of one team leader for every five staff members in a unit and one supervisor for every four team leaders, which covered the personnel needed for a 24-bed floor. Supervisors were selected and trained to coach and mentor.

The results were dramatic. Staff engagement scores rose quickly. And within three months those managers were applying lean thinking, Matt remembers; they were working through A3s to address problems such as bottlenecks in admission and discharge. They were doing time observations and working with staff to identify upstream and downstream issues that affected their process. They were solving their own problems.

"They finally had the time to ask enough *whys*,[48]" Matt says. "That's what changed."

Over time, as we methodically reinstated the supervisory positions, I realized how essential these people are to the lean system. Frontline problems need immediate attention, requiring on-hand experts who are skilled with both lean tools and the work of the unit or clinic.[49] Supervisors are there to help staff members work through problems, teach problem-solving skills, and then, if the issue is too large to handle after 15 minutes, escalating the problem up the chain of command. I have learned that no one can run a lean organization without these small-team leaders.

So, we were not the flat organization we once envisioned. What we were becoming instead was a people-development system. Our first principle in lean healthcare is respecting people. Therefore, our core objective as an organization should be ensuring that people have the

---

48. One very useful tool of the Toyota Production System is called the Five Whys, in which an observer works past assumptions and habits to try to find root cause by asking why a task is done a particular way and then asking *why* four more times. An example is in the appendix, figure 4.

49. At ThedaCare we tried to fill supervisor positions with people who had been through a rotation in the central improvement team, ensuring they were well versed in coaching and leading problem-solving teams.

opportunity to develop skills and knowledge in order to achieve their aspirations.

To truly create that people-development system, we needed to change our processes for teaching, hiring, training, and assessing job performance. Management needed to fully partner with HR instead of just suffering their intrusions. And human resources leaders needed to become more responsive and transparent. HR needed to become lean in order to support a lean organization.

This was driven home for me two years later, when I was touring the Danaher Corporation. Danaher is a collection of science and technology companies known for being one of the earliest adherents of lean thinking.[50] While walking through their offices, I noticed that just about every workstation had a personal development chart displayed somewhere. It showed the competencies that the person was working to acquire, how long he or she had been on that path, and his or her progress.

It is difficult to describe my reaction to seeing this information, which I thought of as deeply personal, displayed so publicly. I was shocked and a little embarrassed for the person named, yet I could not look away. ThedaCare had something we called personal development goals, but it was a list locked away in our personnel files and usually brought out just once a year during the dreaded annual review. We did not discuss our reviews or our goals publicly. It was almost shameful.

Here was my typical annual review: *John, you're a good leader,* but . . . *you intimidate people, you're overbearing, and you don't understand organizational behavior and how people work together.* My personal development goals might be to smile more and stop intimidating people. Try measuring that.

---

50. Danaher Corporation, and its subsidiary Jacobs Vehicle Systems, were featured in the book that is the Rosetta stone for lean and continuous improvement in the United States: "Lean Thinking," by James P. Womack and Daniel T. Jones.

After an hour behind closed doors with my boss, who was focused on finding fault with me, I would be released for another year without further mention of my performance. There was no real mentoring or measuring, no plans for helping me attain my goals. I am surprised we all put up with this system for as long as we did.

Several years and much experimentation later, ThedaCare has a very different assessment and development system that is firmly grounded in data but started out as a casual conversation. Roger Gerard,[51] ThedaCare's chief learning officer for 25 years, tells the story this way: "Jim Matheson, who was our VP of marketing, shared with me that he had a lot of data on our patient population, commissioned from an external source. And I mean *a lot* of data—like a stack of paper a foot thick. Jim said I might be interested in what our patients were saying, and I said, 'Sure.'

"And I read the darn thing," Roger says. "Then I told Jim, 'It's really great that we know now what Lori[52] wants. But if we want 7,000 people to behave to Lori's expectations, we have to figure out what and how to change.'"

So, Roger and Jim put together focus groups from across the ThedaCare system to consider customer needs as shown in the data and discuss how employee behaviors helped or hindered fulfilling those needs. In all, about 500 doctors, nurses, technicians, and administrators from all around northeast Wisconsin participated in the groups. They asked questions like, *What does it mean when patients feel like we are treating their symptoms but not treating them? How can we try to address this?*

---

51. Roger is coauthor with me of *On the Mend* (Lean Enterprise Institute: 2010)

52. "Lori" is the name that ThedaCare employees use to personalize the customer. Lori is not a real person but represents all customers.

Armed with the findings and conclusions of all 30 focus groups, another team then met to break down all that information into four distinct categories. The most common and agreed-upon conclusions of the focus groups were winnowed and set into the proper category. The categories became values, and the common conclusions constituted a list of supporting behaviors. Here are the four main values:

- Put the customer first

- Have a thirst for learning

- Be courageous

- Love our work

The supporting behaviors all serve to define and expand on the values. For instance, under "Be courageous" is "Do what's right. Never ignore things that are wrong" and "Never hide the truth. Let evidence guide the work."

Under "Have a thirst for learning" is "Be willing to be influenced" and "Go and see!"[53]

It was the voice of the customer, filtered and strengthened by ThedaCare's people. These values and behaviors describe the culture ThedaCare is trying to build, so they use it as a guide in hiring people at all levels. In fact, the hiring process at ThedaCare has become more in-depth as it became clear they needed people who care passionately about patient welfare, are team players, *and* are interested in how systems work. Every person who works at ThedaCare will design experiments to improve healthcare delivery and work in teams to solve problems, so it is crucial to hire for these traits.

---

53. The complete Promises/Behavior Guide is available in the appendix, figure 5.

These personal values and behaviors also help managers craft personal development plans and create annual performance assessments. How people will be assessed is no longer a mystery. It is not arbitrary or focused on perceived personal deficits.

"With my direct reports now, instead of looking at what their current gaps are to being an effective leader, we look at what might be potential barriers to attaining the skills or competencies they need," says Brian Burmeister, senior vice president of ThedaCare's now seven hospitals. "It's a complete shift in focus."

Brian, who began his career at ThedaCare as a physical therapist in 1988 and was named president of the hospitals in 2014, calls himself a product of ThedaCare's commitment to people development. But in fact he has also been an important driver of improvement in this area. Even when he was a manager in the era of the flat organization and had more than 100 direct reports, he was committed to meeting with all of them not once but twice a year. That experience led him to understand, however, how futile it was to judge anyone's performance with such an imbalance of managers to staff. "All anyone had to say to me in one of those meetings was, 'How do you know? You're not there when I'm working.' And they would be right."

After the management/staff ratio was corrected, ThedaCare leaders such as Brian and Roger experimented with separating annual performance reviews from development plans entirely, just to be sure that judgment was not getting in the way of development. This created redundancies, however, and complaints about too many meetings. So they returned to one unified assessment and planning session.

At the executive level, Brian conducts personal development sessions with his seven direct reports on a monthly basis. They use self-assessment tools and 360 degree reviews and discuss future goals and how to acquire the skills to meet their aspirations. Some version of this meeting occurs, though usually with less frequency, throughout the organization. Managers, for instance, might meet with their supervisors twice or four times a year to work on a personal development plan. As with Brian, those sessions roll up into the annual performance review. There should be no surprises.

Since expectations are now transparent, it is also possible for the individual goals of staff, and progress toward those goals, to be more transparent. This is the piece of the puzzle that I did not yet understand that day at Danaher: when everyone is moving toward common goals, it becomes less personal and judgmental. When caregivers on a unit are trying to incorporate a new technology or care process, ThedaCare is now far more transparent about displaying the names of team members and checking off everyone's progress toward the goal.

Visual management also extends into the HR department. From a traditional personnel office that closely guarded all information and relied more on sticks than carrots, HR became much more open. The offices now have large, standardized visual management boards. Every job opening and all candidates for positions are posted, as well as each candidate's progress through interviews and skills assessments. Each of the eight recruiters also has visual management boards showing work in progress from initial contact through assessments and interviews. Another board shows the path through career transitions—which is what happens when improvements create the need for staff redeployment—and each person's progress through that standardized redeployment process.

This brings us to another important role for HR in a lean organization: ensuring that there are standardized processes by which promises are kept. The first and most important promise, of course, is that nobody will ever be laid off due to productivity improvements. Lean transformations work only when people feel secure in their employment. Staff members must know that if they improve themselves out of their current job, an equal or better job will be waiting for them. Leaders must make this promise clearly and often. And then teams must create standard work for redeployment so everyone knows exactly what will happen.

In the early days of ThedaCare's transformation, we had not yet thought this through or considered how sensitive people can feel about whether they are wanted or needed. Once, during a rapid-improvement event that included employees in the area being improved, it became clear that it would be much more efficient to handle in-coming phone calls to this outpatient clinic in a different manner. The full-time receptionist would no longer be needed. The woman who was currently in that job—and on the rapid-improvement team—became silent and withdrawn. Someone checked in with HR and found a job that fit the receptionist's skill set, but it was 45 miles away in another town. Deciding that she did not want to commute every day to the other office, the woman quit before an adequate response could be formulated. For months afterward, people scoffed when we said nobody would lose their jobs due to continuous improvement and cited the case of the receptionist.

From this, ThedaCare lean leaders learned that they needed to get out in front of the issue. Now, there is standard work for lean facilitators before a rapid-improvement event that asks whether it is possible that FTEs will be reduced in the improvement area. If so, the facilitator and leaders from the improvement area explain the possible redeployment to area employees long before the high emotion of a rapid-improvement event begins. They ask whether there might be people interested in moving to a different unit or learning a new job. Sometimes volunteers raise a hand immediately, but most people wait until private meetings that are held later.

Leaders meet with employees one-on-one to discuss career goals and opportunities, as well as the needs of the department. Only the best employees are eligible to enter career transitions. Marginally performing employees—those who are struggling with time management, perhaps, or with being an effective team member— must stay and work through their issues with the current manager to ensure that career transitions do not become a dumping ground for problem employees. This does not mean that every high-value employee can leave, of course, or managers would face severe difficulties in getting the work done. Talent juggling and reshuffling of responsibilities within a unit often must happen before eligible employees enter the temporary job pool. Sometimes, people need to wait in temporary assignments for a few months until a new position opens up, and they do so without change in salary or benefits. (A chart depicting this process is in the appendix, figure 6.)

Another promise of lean is that leaders will work hard to make jobs meaningful. Nobody should toil daily at a job that is waste in the process. That would be disrespectful. Fortunately, in the dynamic environment of a lean hospital, opportunities to take on new roles should be more numerous than in a traditional setting. So, helping people develop skills through training and move into new roles become primary jobs of lean HR departments.

None of this is simple, of course. But ThedaCare has been conducting experiments with training and has some interesting results. New hires in nursing used to job shadow an experienced nurse for six months before working independently. Then a team from nursing operations and organizational development created a learning center where new or transitional employees work through simulations. Of course, simulation is not new in clinical training. In the learning center, however, they focus on learning and then repeating the standard work in various roles. They watch experts perform tasks and then do the work while experts observe.

This environment allows for repetition of tasks until they are truly learned, which is difficult or impossible while working with real patients on a unit. Rather than shadowing a nurse on a real unit for six months, nurses who go through the learning center have been fully trained and nearly independent on the floor within two months. This greatly facilitates the organization's ability to move nurses to new assignments as improvement activities change the needs for skills in each unit.

The next experiment will be to simulate standard work in the learning center for new managers. Physicians are also beginning to explore how they can make use of the learning center for new hires or introduce independent physicians to the ThedaCare operating system.

Throughout this chapter, without using the word, morale has been the focus. Because morale and engagement are critical in the lean world— where nobody can pretend that anything can be accomplished without the help and support of frontline staff—leaders have spent a lot of time studying this. What makes a person become more interested in his or her work? What causes people to disengage and become careless?

Over time, ThedaCare leadership identified staffing mix as the biggest driver in employee satisfaction and engagement scores. When the right number of nurses with the right expertise was on the floor responding to that day's patient volume, people were happy. Leaders knew this because they started asking every nurse on every shift the simple question, "Are you having a good day?"[54] For months they asked and tracked the responses on a chart, using red dots when the answer was no and green dots for yes.

The year 2014 was both great and confusing for morale studies. In the northeast of Wisconsin, winter hits hard and stays for a long time.

---

54. Nurses understood that they were being asked whether they were stressed from overwork and whether they were being pushed outside their level of competency.

Our flu seasons can be epic. But they are usually just a season. We have spikes of heavy traffic from late December through March, and then it tapers off. It tapers either quickly or slowly, but it tapers. Not in 2014. ThedaCare was still riding that high tide of patient admissions into late summer without any relief in sight.

At the same time, Kim Barnas, then president of ThedaCare hospitals, and her teams were also working on staffing issues. For nurses, getting the right shift and being able to leave on time are huge drivers of job satisfaction. When staffing models do not meet needs, leaders were often obliged to resort to force-overs.[55] So getting the staffing mix is a critical and emotional issue.

During a period when everyone expected nursing demand to drop—due to the end of flu season and new outpatient procedures that allowed more people to heal at home—Kim's team began trying new models. So, the tests were a little more stressful than usual but still instructive.

First, they experimented with having nurses flex across a couple of units, filling in one day in the ICU or obstetrics, for instance, before returning to a medical unit. Over the years, however, there had been an increase in specialized tasks for nurses in these units, so a highly regarded OB nurse probably does not know how to perform many ICU tasks. Therefore, the visiting nurse in the ICU was out of her comfort zone and being treated as a nurses' aid. This led to much dissatisfaction.

"We realized that it was disrespectful to everyone involved," Kim says. "People were not being developed into roles, and many of them felt lost."

They went back to studying the data and talking to nurses about their days. The team then experimented with creating a dual staffing system. Every unit would have a core staff, deep in expertise that would

---

55. A force-over is when a nurse is required to work hours past his or her shift in order to cover for staffing shortages or in the face of spikes in patient volume.

change rarely. They would also have flex staffers who would be paid more to develop necessary expertise on three or four units. Becoming a flex staffer would be a choice, and it would come with additional training and pay.

But they ran up against another issue: many different units and clinics across the hospital had different start times. One unit might begin days at 6:30 a.m. while, two floors down, a specialty unit might always start at 7 a.m. Kim's team decided that, to make flex staffing work for those who were willing to move around, every unit needed to start their shifts at the same time.

"This was another big lesson that we learned," Kim says. "Shift start times are really important to people. They have all kinds of responsibilities in the mornings, like getting kids fed and ready for school. Even a half-hour change can really mess up a schedule. We rolled out this change all at once, and there was anxiety and chaos all over the place. We should have moved much more slowly and done a proof of concept first."

Even when trying to create a system that treats people more respectfully, Kim found, it was possible to overlook the needs of the very people you are trying to respect. This can be just as damaging to morale as those force-overs.

ThedaCare continues to experiment with ways to respond to spikes and valleys in patient volume while keeping productivity within a reasonable range. As most people in healthcare realize, this is one of the biggest challenges hospitals currently face. With changes in insurance mechanisms and sometimes wildly fluctuating populations and healthcare options, everyone needs to be flexible. This is a critical area of experimentation, and the fact that ThedaCare's work in this area continued in 2014 even as top leadership in the hospital changed—when Brian became president of the hospitals division upon Kim's departure—is testament to succession planning.

Which brings us to our final topic in the subject of developing people: succession planning. A good succession plan is critical to a lean healthcare system both as a promise and a development tool.

The promise is what the leaders make to the people and to each another: that the lean improvement efforts will continue past the current administration. A robust succession plan—one that includes training for candidates and emphasizes lean skills—clearly signals that putting effort into improvement now will lead to advancement. Lean improvement work is not easy. A succession plan says, "Put in the effort now and you will be rewarded."

The development piece of succession planning is both personal and system-wide. As CEO of ThedaCare, I had a short list of candidates for my job, as well as a list of skills I thought necessary for the job. Each candidate was rated on those skills and then given opportunities to develop where needed. Each candidate in turn created development plans for the candidates for his or her job. Succession planning is really skills-development planning for the whole system. This is what Dr. Thomas Hansen, CEO of Seattle Children's, calls "bench strength"—knowing that you have people prepared to step in and do the next job up.

This requires some planning. When Tom left the top spot at Columbus Children's Hospital in Ohio in 2005 to join Seattle Children's, he began succession planning right away. He started with a list of the experience, skills, and capabilities required of a CEO—all culled from the public job description Seattle Children's had used to hire him—and found a couple of candidates. Once he knew who his candidates were, he could compare their skills and experience with the list and make a plan to help each one fulfill the list.[56]

"One of the things we're looking for, for instance, is a person with experience working with physicians and scientists in clinical, education, and research capacities. And that might be a challenge for some of our internal folks because the research scientists work in a different building downtown. They won't bump into each other in the hallways," Tom says.

"So, it's my job to create opportunities for my candidates to work with scientists in the research facility. Candidates also need to have extensive experience with CPI,[57] and an outsider isn't going to have that. It might take five years to get there, so these are necessarily long-term plans."

At Seattle Children's, every executive at the level of vice president and above has a plan to fill his or her job. Each person identifies two or more candidates for the job, lists the skills and experience the candidate needs to fill the roll, and creates a plan to help the person get what he or she needs. A readiness time frame—from now to five years out—is also noted.[58]

Every six months, the Management Development Succession committee of the board of trustees reviews and approves everyone's candidates and plans. Every year the plans are presented to the board. Final hiring decisions are left to the board, of course, but at least Tom can now answer the questions that trustees have been known to ask, such as: *What happens if you get hit by a bus? What happens if the chief development officer retires suddenly?*

---

56. See Tom's succession plan in the appendix, figure 7.

57. Continuous Performance Improvement, CPI, is the name of Seattle Children's improvement system.

58. A standardized form used by Seattle Children's is in the appendix, figure 8.

"I view this as part of our retention plan, too, because if people know they are in the line of succession, that's a real statement about our commitment to them," Tom says.

As part of succession-plan review, Tom and the hiring committee also keep a close eye on diversity in the workforce. It is important that the patients see themselves represented in the people who are caring for them, Tom says. When succession planning is standardized for the top few layers of management, it becomes easier to look across the field— down to candidates just beginning their careers in management—and be intentional about tomorrow's leadership.

We depend on HR to partner with us in operations in many new ways once we start down a lean path. The same is true for finance, where we have completely reformed relationships and found value where we never expected.

8

Lean
Finance

Accountants have a bad reputation. Rumored to be humorless and tight fisted, they are encountered by most healthcare managers just once a year during the annual budget exercise. This is the season in which operations folks are asked to guess what they will need in the coming year. Everyone inflates their numbers knowing that finance will give 25% less and then complains that the process is arbitrary. Then the finance department puts the annual budget into black and white as if it were set in stone and holds everyone's feet to the fire when they stray from last year's best guess.

We are the ones saving lives, we say to each other on the operations side. Finance should support the lean transformation instead of bossing us around and creating barriers. And we are right, of course. So, it is time that operations let finance become partners in this business of providing better patient care.

As it stands, most finance professionals have been relegated to the roles of auditors, enforcers, and cops. These are people trained to see patterns in numbers, to interpret data in ways few of us can fathom, and to actually foresee future problems. Yet people in operations often treat them like a nuisance.

It is time to redefine the true purpose of the finance department as a partner in lean operations, providing expertise in interpreting and translating the numbers. Finance professionals bring a unique point of view to identifying and addressing problems and should be represented on every possible improvement team. Leaders need them practicing at the top of their skill set, helping everyone to see problems lurking in the data, dangers around the bend. Instead of cops, they should be the organization's uncursed Cassandras.[59]

In lean systems, the P&L for each unit, clinic, or product family is under the control of an area manager or director.[60] Because unit managers are often talented nurses or therapists, they usually arrive at the job without a business background. They are given some training, of course, but what they really need is ongoing support. At ThedaCare and many other lean healthcare organizations, that support comes in the form of leadership teams created for every hospital unit and outpatient clinic. These leadership teams include advisors from finance, HR, information technology, and any other specialty the line manager might need to effectively run his or her small business, including the continuous-improvement work. These teams act like a trusted executive team, with the manager as CEO. Membership can change with the unit's changing needs, but the finance member is almost always a key player, there to assist with the P&L and various cost analyses and to help the manager see emerging facts and trends.

---

59. In Greek mythology, Cassandra is given the gift of prophecy, but after spurning Apollo's advances, she is cursed so that she is never believed.

60. In this and other examples, managers are in the middle of a five-layer organizational structure that includes chief executives, vice presidents and directors, managers, supervisors, and shift leads. Managers in a lean health system often have chief-executive responsibilities for their unit or product family.

At this point, I can see CFOs and finance managers shaking their heads and asking, "Where are we going to find the time and capacity to be advisors and consultants throughout the organization?" The answer: you will stop wasting time by creating, arguing over, and policing an annual budget.

Creating a budget is a major exercise in waste. The moment it is written on paper, it is obsolete. So you spend an entire year trying to reconcile the current reality against what you thought might happen six or nine or 12 months earlier—an exercise that hardly offers new information about the state of your business. Creating a budget causes ongoing fights between managers, who want more resources, and the accountants, who want everyone to stick to seemingly arbitrary numbers. For decades, everyone accepted the discord because the budget process was said to be necessary.

When I was with ThedaCare, the budget seemed to me an excuse for raising expenses every year. Rather than focusing on improving performance, managers and executives concentrated on spending everything in their budgets in the hope that next year, they would not have to make do with less. It is no wonder that expenses rose faster than revenues some years.

Instead of an annual budget, I strongly recommend that health systems adopt a forecasting system. Forecasting is an estimate of likely future outcomes. It is where leaders think that the organization is heading, adjusted quarterly as new facts emerge. It is a far more accurate gauge of what will happen next quarter—what you will need in terms of resources and the amount of revenue you will likely pull in—and, yet, in every company I know of that has switched to forecasting, it requires less time to prepare.

A budget requires you to address the big question—*Where are we heading?* —once a year. A forecast allows everyone to look into the future at least once a quarter.

The critical work of a forecast is determining which factors actually drive the business and then setting up standard work to collect and input those drivers on a regular basis. Data on every driver should autopopulate into the forecast, and drivers must be reviewed and agreed upon. Drivers are not 7,000 lines of data as on the spreadsheets that make up the budget. Drivers are the few forces that will make or break a business, such as nursing hours per patient day or number of surgeries per day.[61]

A budget and a forecast will also provoke very different behaviors in staff. Once a year, a budget demands that managers and executives make a 12-month assumption that bends resources in their favor. Then throughout the year, the budget focuses managers' attention on reaching a set of negotiated targets. It encourages blame over investigation. It is just too easy to say, "Bill didn't hit his numbers; he's a bad manager."

A forecast is a report of what people believe or know will happen in the coming months based on historical evidence and known facts, such as flu season begins and salary increases take effect for 30% of employees. Nobody is trying to hit the numbers of the forecast; nobody gets reprimanded when the flu season is heavier than expected. Forecasts are simple facts about the foreseeable future.

Targets are separate from the forecast. Targets are aspirational; forecasts are factual. That clear distinction between targets and forecasts is what makes forecasting this system ideal for an organization dedicated to continuous improvement.

"A budget is the result of negotiations. So it is a bunch of negotiated targets that are based on annual assumptions. It often fails to reflect reality," says Steve Player, program director for the Beyond Budgeting

---

61. Number of surgeries per day is a valid driver only as long as we exist in a fee-for-service world. If we make the switch to risk-adjusted global payments, a driver might be number of avoidable hospital admissions.

Round Table in North America.[62] "The real power of forecasting is in the fact the forecasts are realistic and targets are aspirational. The forecast is never bent in order to meet a target. Instead, leaders study the gaps between forecast and target for improvement opportunities.

"Being able to see the gap between forecast and target means I can see and understand my company's real performance. Then, I can take steps to close the gap between current performance and target," Player says.

Like Rachelle Schultz and Winona Health Systems from chapter 1, ThedaCare now keeps a rolling forecast that shows four quarters in the past and six quarters into the future. The past is used to help extrapolate into the future. Both Winona and ThedaCare executives have found that six quarters into the future is about as far as they can go while maintaining accuracy. Both organizations update the forecast quarterly.

At ThedaCare, leaders in operations and finance have an ongoing dialogue that begins with a weekly meeting to review key performance indicators, looking at what drives cost and revenue in the system. Executives from finance and operations might decide to track nursing hours worked across the system, for instance, while trying to better understand the financial consequences of different staffing models.

Brian McGinnis, ThedaCare's vice president of finance, checks key performance indicators daily and meets with directors and managers in operations every week to review these business drivers.[63] They talk about what happened last week, review trends in the data, and talk about new forces that might affect spending and revenue. Every month,

---

62. Player is also coauthor, with Steve Morlidge, of *Future Ready: How to Master Business Forecasting* (John Wiley & Sons, 2010)

63. Drivers and key performance indicators can be synonymous. In general, key performance indicators are the agreed-upon metrics being used to track certain aspects of the business, such as staffing hours, while business drivers are more broad categories such as revenue per FTE or cost of quality.

there is a management-reporting meeting to discuss how the entire health system did against the targets.

"We are always comparing what was forecast with what actually happened as a way to build internal intelligence," says McGinnis, who joined the system in 2012 from a public accounting firm. "We're always trying to improve the way that we spot trends and respond. We're always seeking ways to separate the signal from the noise."

And noise is everywhere in company finances. A physician's month-long absence from a rural clinic can cause revenue to plummet and produce reactions that are inappropriate when the physician returns, such as cutting staff hours to make up for the decline in revenue. Meanwhile, signals that need our attention, such as a growing number of cases of influenza among people who received an annual vaccine, remain hidden in the noise of a conventional budgeting process.

The idea is that financial analysts should be in constant communication with operations, collecting intelligence from the front line and then showing and explaining the data trends that result from daily decisions.

"What we're looking for is a continuous flow from monthly reporting to quarterly forecasting, when we get together and ask whether what we learned in the last quarter changed our ideas of what will happen in the next six quarters," says McGinnis.

This focus on the gap between what people thought would happen and what did happen keeps everyone attentive to improvement opportunities. And keeping eyes on the future gives leaders time to create thoughtful responses to big changes instead of simply winging it.

Another reason to lose the budget: it is expensive to produce. McGinnis says ThedaCare was spending about 20,000 hours every year creating a budget, largely due to the fact that every line item in the budget was the result of sometimes-lengthy negotiations. Quarterly forecasts, populated by simple facts and projections, require just 2,500 hours per year. The finance department has reinvested those hours back into the business, mostly in the cause of assisting managers, directors, and other leaders as they improve the business.

It is important to note, however, that as notoriously unhelpful as the budget is, it is deeply embedded in our habits and expectations. It will not go quietly into that good night. If you plan for a few battles and take small, steady steps, you can put it where it belongs: in your rearview mirror.

Rachelle Schultz and her leadership team at Winona Health Systems began their transition from budgets to forecasting with a simple wish: to have the same kind of timely data for the whole system that they got for improvement projects. Financial data in the form of dusty old budgets stuck out like a sore thumb, and people were frustrated with how much time they spent calculating variances.

At the same time, in 2011, a consulting company that worked with Winona was building an early version of forecasting software for healthcare. Rachelle and her team tested it out and then agreed to be a beta site. They ran trials, trained finance staff in using the software, created standard work surrounding the forecasting inputs, and then started running financial reports and offering feedback to the software engineers. Together, they focused the software to give them what they needed.

Next, Rachelle began talking with board members about her vision of the forecasting approach. She made the case that their budget was always out of date and more trouble than it was worth. They spent more time explaining variances than they did exploring and responding to new business realities. The board agreed to a trial. For one year, Winona would run two systems—traditional budgets and forecasting—side by side to get a sense of the strengths and weaknesses of each.

The Winona leadership team then set financial targets, such as days cash on hand, accounts receivable days, operating margin, and revenue per FTE. The team created forecasts for those targets running six quarters out, based on past performance and the changes that they knew would be coming, such as new reimbursement rules for Medicare and a new surgeon joining the hospital, bringing new costs and revenue streams. For every gap between a target and a forecast, they used A3 thinking and created countermeasures, often in the form of team-based improvement projects.

Meanwhile, Rachelle began preparing managers and accountants to work more closely together. "We started having our managers and directors meet with their accountant regularly to better understand finance and learn how to utilize forecasting," Rachelle says.

Each accountant was assigned to an area of operations, such as cancer care or convalescent services, and met monthly with every manager in that area to talk about what was happening and what they foresaw. Those monthly meetings rolled up into quarterly meetings with senior executives. Using frontline intelligence, senior executives could make adjustments to the forecast.

That first year running the budgeting process and forecasting side by side was challenging but necessary, Rachelle says. They needed a full year of good reporting, anyway, to create the four-quarters-back, six-quarters-forward rolling forecast they wanted. So, the finance department was essentially running old and new reports side by side and working to improve their process with each iteration.

Meanwhile, leaders in finance and operations were running experiments. They scheduled the type of meetings they would need to select and capture appropriate forecasting information, created standard work around the meetings and tasks, tested it, and adjusted as necessary. Every quarter was an iteration to learn more about what they needed and when, in terms of feeding good information into the system.

By the end of the year, finance members had become adept at running both systems, but Rachelle would caution anyone about getting relaxed there. When the board approved her move to forecasting only, she stopped issuing budgets before people got too comfortable having both systems and started clinging to the old ways like a security blanket. It would have been like using paper patient records even after you have gone digital, she says. The chance of overlap errors and the ongoing waste of duplicated effort are too great.

Instead, she kept everyone focused on perfecting the forecasting process, creating standard work, and then checking back to see whether the standard work was being followed and whether it needed to be adjusted. In the three years since Winona Health Systems stopped producing a budget, there has been no regret, Rachelle says. In fact, they have learned to forecast not just financials but also safety, patient satisfaction, and quality.

"For example, we have a small rural clinic where a provider left. We recruited another, but that new physician could not start work for some number of months, and we knew that we were going to have to close that clinic a couple of days a week, and that is a big dissatisfier. We saw our results go down, but we knew they would," Rachelle says. "So we could plan for that and then plan for how we would build the patient satisfaction back up for that clinic."

Keeping everyone's eyes trained on the target and the forecast in these areas means they are always looking for countermeasures. And that feeds back into improvement efforts that are focused on the future. McGinnis calls it "looking out the front windows of the business."

At the same time, chief executives such as Rachelle have that forward-looking visibility throughout the system, along with the flexibility of quarterly adjustments to their forecasts. For example, let's say that, as CEO, you know two big things are likely to happen in the next fiscal year: a large group of your orthopedic surgeons are making noise about splitting off to open their own surgery center and you have just sealed the deal to become the main provider on two new insurance plans that will phase in throughout the year. How do you respond?

In a budgeting system, you would probably front-load the necessary new personnel to create capacity for all those new patients coming with the insurance plans. If the primary care clinic will require 24 new RNs and MAs, that goes into the annual budget, and the clinic is prompted to hire and train two dozen new people right away. This sort of batch hiring is full of potential problems, not least of which is the fact that you do not need all of these people right away and are not entirely sure that 24 is the right number. In a forecasting system, you would likely plan a phased hire-in over three or four quarters. This would allow you to improve on each iteration of hiring and training and avoid the cost of extra salaries until there is more certainty about the effect of the new insurance contract on patient volumes. Also, you might be able to move some of those RNs from orthopedics to primary care, thus retaining your skilled nurses.

Moving from budgeting to forecasting will be a radical idea for some people, but taking methodical steps toward the goal will help reassure those who feel unsettled. If I were to plan a move from budgeting to forecasting today, based on the ThedaCare experience and what I have learned from other providers such as Winona, I would do these five things in order.

1. Begin working with division leaders and other executives to prepare for forecasting—not with spreadsheets and finance

lectures but with strategy sessions. First, I would schedule quarterly meetings with all division heads to discuss their businesses, including what they want to achieve over the next two or three quarters, the realities they foresee, and how each executive can best align with the organization's overall strategy. Look carefully at recent cost and quality trends and talk about any coming changes to revenue streams, costs, or ability to compete. Forecasting is all about understanding the basic rhythms of the business. This will be a mind-set adjustment for people in operations; some may need to be convinced that you are not there to chastise them about adherence to the budget. Prepare to be patient.

2. Talk to your board about the benefits of forecasting and bring in experts—even from other industries—to describe life without the annual budget.[64] Ask board members what information they want most and then be prepared to show how forecasting will deliver it. At ThedaCare, we invited Orry Fiume, one of the authors of the seminal text in lean finance, to speak to the board, and he was a very positive influence.

3. Finance leaders should create the forecasting process they plan to use and then write standard work for it. There is no off-the-shelf software that will do forecasting for you. As Rachelle Schultz will tell you, software can help, but it cannot implement the standard work and systemic changes needed to make forecasting work. What is important here is to create the system-wide plan—using standard work—to support forecasting. The CFO should present this standard work to the senior management team to build familiarity with the system.

---

64. One good resource is the Beyond Budgeting Round Table at bbrtna.org. The book that most influenced my thinking is *Real Numbers: Management Accounting in a Lean Organization* by Jean E. Cunningham and Orest J. Fiume.

4. Make the new practices visual. Large process maps should be posted in the finance department that detail what goes into a forecast and how it is configured, as well as samples of forecasting's end products. Every member of the finance department should be able to use these maps to explain the new practices.

5. Plan for the gaps (aka red ink). For most companies, finances will occasionally slip into negative territory. Create a clear process for dealing with it. This is an opportunity to study and adjust, to use the A3 to delve more deeply into the hidden realities and relationships that create red ink. Emphasize studying the process over finding fault with people.

Reimagining the role of the finance department does not stop at replacing budgets with forecasting, of course. The goal here is to release finance professionals from the tedium of repetitive, wasteful tasks so that they can join operations teams as advisors. So, what is the next rote task that can be eliminated?

"The monthly close," says McGinnis. "The month is over. It is old news. But everybody goes through the ritual of the close because that's what we do. At this point, we spend 700 hours a month at ThedaCare closing the books. That's 8,400 hours a year. We will be doing rapid-improvement events in 2015 and hope to work that number down to 2,400 hours a year. But that doesn't change the fact that it is an exercise in waste."

The problem with the monthly close, McGinnis likes to say, is in the underlying assumption that there is some magical change in circumstance from April to May or from September to October. As if moving from the thirtieth of the month to the first means that whatever happened in April is no longer relevant. Viewing finances based on dates of the calendar instead of by real circumstances—a bulge in stroke cases, a mass exodus of orthopedic surgeons—skews our understanding of cause and effect.

When organizations free their financial analysts from the usual monthly and annual reports, analysts have time to help find and answer more interesting questions. What is the correlation between nursing hours per patient day and patient satisfaction? How do we separate the signal from the noise on that issue? And why does revenue per patient visit in the clinics go wonky every third quarter?

The challenge, McGinnis says, is finding out what executives and board members really want. A lot of leaders are accustomed to those monthly reports. The columns and numbers are as comfortable as old slippers and can even feel like real information. People might cling to the old ways. So McGinnis meets with leaders and gently points out that the monthly close is backward looking and expensive to produce and asks, "What information are you really looking for here? What would you most like to see?" Then, he tries to accommodate that. As of spring 2015, McGinnis was still doing the monthly close but still hoping to relegate that activity to history.

The promise of the digital age, which lean finance seeks to fully capture, is real-time information delivered in the most useful format at the speed of light, personalized, relevant, and accurate. However, healthcare has not just been behind in redefining its need for financial information but also lagged in exploiting the potential of new information technologies more generally. So there is another partnership we need to create and strengthen. It is time to shake hands with IT.

9

Clinical
Business Intelligence

Using data to drive decision making is a common enough goal for businesses in the first quarter of the twenty-first century. Organizations claim to be governed by facts and that data lead the way. As a corporate advertisement, it sounds great. As anyone who has actually tried to do this knows, it gets complicated fast.

As it turns out, all of those facts that an organization needs in order to build a meaningful picture of business and clinical operations are being collected and controlled in many departments. When you think about it, it is not surprising. Data are locked into separate silos in a mirror image of most organizations and mind-sets.

Therefore, I am sorry to say, this chapter is not so much about killer apps—although I have seen a few—as it is about how to think about data and the flow of information for a lean transformation. You will need the right mind-set before addressing your skill sets and, finally, your tool sets.

At ThedaCare and other organizations such as Salem Health in Oregon's capital city, leaders have spent years experimenting with different ways to systematize and move data to support a lean organization. What we have found will offer a glimpse into the kind of clinical and business results that are possible when you begin at the beginning.

When I was chief medical officer at ThedaCare, I remember trying to get timely, integrated information out of our systems. As one of the first healthcare organizations in the country to adopt electronic medical records (in the mid-1990s), we knew that we had advanced software systems that were sucking up all kinds of data about every patient we treated and billed. We wanted to pose questions to the data such as, "Is there a correlation between surgical infections and nursing staff levels in postoperative care?" and get a meaningful answer.

Instead, we were sent from one office to the next. We would get cost information from one source and then walk down the hall to get clinical information, and it was off to another department for productivity information. The reports rarely matched up enough to give us a clear picture. It was like we had asked three different questions instead of one.

So, in 1999 I started a new department called Decision Resources. Staffed with about 32 computer analysts whom I hired or stole from finance, quality, and clinical operations, they learned from each other how we could use information to support frontline and back-office business and clinical decisions. This new department was not part of, or reporting to, Information Technology (IT) because I did not want to confuse our search for information with the kind of hardware and software solutions for payroll, payables, insurance billing, regulatory compliance, electronic health records, etc., that were the IT bread and butter.

Decision Resources produced some terrific reports, integrating information from many sources so that the answers were responding to the same question. Executives and managers began pulling for more, even though reports took four to six weeks to complete. It was not long before those Decision Resources analysts showed up for work every day to face down an enormous backlog. If we had 50 more analysts, we would still have had a backlog.

In 2002, we hired a consultant named Brian Veara and asked him to address the bottleneck. Brian came with extensive experience in analytics and project management at very large retail and manufacturing organizations. Under his leadership, Decision Resources improved productivity and standardized some of the reports, but the department still could not keep up with demand.

The demand for data and information was increasing because ThedaCare's people were asking new types of analytical questions, focused on measuring the processes of clinical care. This was dramatically different from the way healthcare organizations traditionally measured their performance. Historically, reporting was focused on the external requirements for health plans, the government agencies, and regulatory compliance. So, Brian's team went out to their customers— all of the staff, managers, directors, and executives who were requesting specific reports—and asked, "What information do you really need here in order to take action? What problems are you trying to solve?"

This is the moment we began to evolve from an organization that reacts to one that anticipates, and our analysts began the journey from being report writers to partners. After all, analysts are like finance auditors and HR experts in that they have specialized knowledge to bring to the table. So, instead of taking orders from folks in operations, analysts should be looking at issues alongside line managers in order to anticipate their information needs.

As part of this evolution, we knew we needed to set larger goals that were not limited in scope by current technology. We were thinking of how we were going to serve the evolving continuous-improvement agenda of operations. So, we said that our goal was to create a system that collects and analyzes data and delivers up-to-date results to front-line clinicians to help them make better decisions and take action. We called the system Clinical Business Intelligence (CBI), and the idea was that people on the front line would use the system to know everything from the current inpatient infection rate to whether units are over- or understaffed. People could then base improvement efforts on current facts rather than hunches or organizational lore.

Eventually, we found a few other healthcare organizations that were also trying to integrate their data streams and make them relevant to the front line. Together, we have now created a learning network of nearly two dozen health systems that share experiments and knowledge in this area.[65]

Using our collective experiences through the CBI network, I can now describe a common trajectory for healthcare organizations that are learning to integrate data collection with lean improvement efforts. It begins with realizing that there is no external software solution for this work.

Let me correct that. There are plenty of software "solutions" out there and lots of vendors who will tell you that they have a product that is a perfect fit for your needs. You will need to tweak your expectations and work processes only a little bit to interact seamlessly with this new system, the salespeople tell you.. And in three years when it is time to upgrade to a new version or replace the now-unsupported software, you will need to change your processes and expectations again to fit the language and logic of the new software. At which point we need to ask, who is serving whom? As my colleague Julie Bartels[66] likes to say, "We don't want a vendor driving our culture."

---

65. A more complete description of the Clinical Business Intelligence Network is available at the back of this book, in the endnotes.

66. Julie is the Program Manager, Wisconsin State Health Innovation Plan, EVP, ThedaCare Center for Healthcare Value.

Health systems that are serious about continuous improvement need to build their own measurement systems to ensure that the patient stays at the center of the equation. An organization's clinical business intelligence system should be able to accurately inform the organization how well clinical and operational processes are performing. The detail of the data needs to be at the level that can expose the process steps that are not performing well. Only then can a process owner take action and measure the impact of process changes. A vendor's clinical business intelligence solution is too generic and not capable of exposing the process steps without significant time and costly modifications.[67]

When initiating any large project like this one, people in a lean organization begin by investigating and mapping the current state. One of the first questions to ask is "Where are the data coming from?" If you are like most healthcare companies, the majority of your data is most likely produced by or filtered through the finance or quality departments. It is a widespread logic that finance will have the most complete and accurate information because it captures data in order to produce an accurate bill.

The trouble is that a lot of important activity falls outside of the invoice. At ThedaCare we discovered that productivity-related data in a clinic were often wildly inaccurate because of delays in the billing processes and because not every activity is billed. The billing process requires coding and sometimes transcription before a bill is created. This can take days or weeks to complete. The closer we looked, the more we realized that the lag time between when an event occurred and when the data were posted by finance was a real problem if we wanted up-to-date information.

---

67. Not all packaged software systems are bad, of course. CBI efforts need software such as QlikView, a data integrator that sits on top of all of an organization's legacy systems to extract information. We just cannot expect packaged software to do the hard work of organizing our information infrastructure.

"At ThedaCare, even some of the quality reporting was influenced by the post date," Brian says. "The report might show a February readmission happening in March because that is when the account was financially posted. People would look at it and think, 'We didn't have a readmission in March.' So, the data were considered unreliable."

To address this issue, Brian's team worked closely with people in finance to create new expectations for how data should flow. Together, they removed chokepoints and reassigned some responsibilities. Only then could they begin addressing even thornier issues, such as the fact that ThedaCare often had five different definitions for common terms such as "length of stay" in its hospitals.

When we talk to people about how to begin a CBI effort, we begin by explaining that the starting line is several steps back from where they imagined. "The first step," Julie Bartels always says, "is finding a champion for the new initiative in the C-suite."

If the CEO or COO is not leading this effort, an improvement team leader should be looking for a specific project that will interest an executive sponsor, even as the team begins untangling data sources and mapping the current state. There is usually some low-hanging fruit—an issue or roadblock that, once corrected, will have a sizable impact— in the early days of this type of initiative. Find one of interest to the sponsor and use it to illustrate the power of integrated, up-to-date intelligence. These early projects might not be elegant, but addressing a specific problem helps keep a team focused even as the list of issues and questions regarding the larger effort mounts higher.

Once a sponsor is on board, take a team and *go see*. Find out which health systems are delivering actionable intelligence to the front line and go learn from them. Look for ideas you can re-create in your own system, and listen carefully for the cautionary tales. Every organization that has achieved a level of excellence with CBI has a list of mistakes in its past. Ask leaders what they would have done differently.

Now, it is time to define what you want to do with all those possibilities you have uncovered. With your team, set your CBI strategy. This should be more than a statement of intent, Brian says. The strategy should include:

- Who owns the work, the strategy, and the road map for CBI; who is accountable

- What is the scope of CBI—what is included and excluded from the program

- The objectives and initial measures for CBI

As part of this formalization, the team should create a measureable intake process for all CBI requests. (Be sure to read the Salem Health story below before imagining this is a standardized form to fill out.) Also, the team should be talking about how they might measure the value of their work.

Transparency of the work is paramount to the initiative's success. You need to build a marketing or communications effort into the work to ensure that you are broadcasting to sponsors—and to the organization at large—what you are aiming for and what you achieve. Be prepared to tell people what problems are being solved and why this work is important. This will prepare your colleagues outside of CBI for the coming changes and help to create the right mind-set in the organization.

Next, define your team's working structure. Will it be centralized or decentralized or a hybrid? Who will be full-time, part-time, or ad hoc? Be clear on how the team will communicate and interface with the larger organization. Think function over form.

The team should then establish a master data management program. This includes establishing the key fields, tables, metrics, and dimensions you will use, as well as determining who owns the information and how it will be sourced. This must be a formal process, with an owner and a small steering committee.

Now it is time to establish an information governance program to lay out data definitions, HIPPA and privacy, latency and currency of information, and accuracy. In other words, determine how the information will be used. Like the master data management program, the information governance program will need a written charter, a mission, and clear objectives and metrics, such as turnaround time. All governance should be very nimble.

Let's take a specific example of how the CBI team can build a case and change the thinking of an important audience. One issue Brian and his team at ThedaCare worked through involved stubbornly high per-surgery costs. With so many variables in each surgery and with surgeons accustomed to controlling supplies and procedures, finding and correcting cost variations are difficult for any organization.

Still, data can speak much louder than words. A team analyzed data associated with the surgeries of all providers and discovered that some surgeons were using more expensive glue for spinal cord surgery. It was interesting but would not impress surgeons. So the executive leader of the spine care improvement work at ThedaCare, Shawn Chartier, and the analytical team partnered with some influential spine surgeons and pulled clinical outcomes data into the mix. They used detailed surgical data comparing physicians on equivalent patient types to prove that there was no difference in patient outcomes related to the different types of glue. The only variance was cost.

Chartier was then able to present the case to surgeons for using the less costly glue as the standard. The agreement was not immediate, of course, but all providers did eventually switch to the standard glue. This saved ThedaCare $650,000 a year and delivered a clear illustration of the power of clinical business intelligence.

"We could not achieve results of this importance if we were sitting back waiting for people to ask us to produce reports," Brian says. "CBI is not about reporting. Reporting itself is wasteful if not used to take action. It is about collaborating with operations to drive improvement."

Sara Iodice will agree with that statement. At Salem Health, where Iodice is director of technology, they talked about data reporting as being inside a magic box. They did not want unit managers or other leaders asking for specific reports or tools. Instead, they wanted to have longer conversations with their colleagues in operations, focused on problems they were trying to address, in order to let the business intelligence team pick the best tool to meet the needs.

"Before we started down this road, we did a business intelligence maturity assessment on our people, processes, and tools and found that our processes scored the lowest, with technology being the most mature. We just needed to address how we thought about and approached the data," Iodice says. "So we began focusing with people on what they wanted to do with the information. We would say, 'Don't tell me what reports you want. That's in the magic box. Just tell me what problems you want to solve.'"

In 2013, shortly after they formally began their CBI program, the problem they heard about was with central-line infections. Salem Health, a community-based not-for-profit system of two hospitals and several clinics that sees about 93,000 emergency room visits a year, was averaging one central-line infection every month, and the numbers were going in the wrong direction. Leaders tagged the issue for an improvement project and the business intelligence team was asked to join in and bring the magic box.

Together, team members broke down the central-line process into a few important components: decision to place the line, ordering the line, and documentation of reasons. Early on, it was clear that documentation of the procedure was inconsistent, so it was difficult to spot what was happening.

The team created standardized reporting, trained frontline staff in keeping records, and pushed all reports through the business intelligence team. Any time a central line was placed in a patient without a written order, an order was incomplete, or the line was ordered for an uncommon reason, team members investigated the circumstances and gave training on correct procedures.

"One failure we found was in the standardized nursing documentation on central lines. There was no reporting of how the site was prepped or how often it was cleaned because it wasn't part of the original documentation," Jason Stark, business intelligence manager at Salem Health says. "Changing that had a big impact."

When incidence of central-line infections fell dramatically, clinical staff decided that they needed to be certain of the reason. For months, they tracked every slight spike in temperature for everyone who had a central line and ran tests to be certain there was no infection. Within six months of beginning the new standard work on ordering, placing, prepping, and cleaning central lines in February 2014, the rate of infection fell to zero.

"It used to be that people would come and ask for reports. Now, we're partnering more with people in quality and in our improvement offices," Iodice says, "because data alone are not going to transform care."

The next step for Salem Health will probably be toward greater velocity, if Brian Veara's experience holds true. First, get the mind-set and skill sets in place, he says. Then use the tools and increase the volume.

For instance, when Brian was satisfied that there was a strong collaborative relationship between information analysts and operations managers, he began thinking about how to get people the information they needed, even faster. He still wanted managers and executives to have the kind of open-ended conversations they were having about problems, but he saw a need to get out of the way when it came to standard reporting, especially on key performance indicators.

Thinking about the increasingly popular self-serve and on-demand markets, Brian started working out ways that people could reach out and grab their own key metrics. It would be like teaching someone to take his or her own pulse. He considered delivering real-time data but said that real-time data can often be like drinking out of a fire hose. The volume and velocity are not helpful.

In the end, Brian and his team designed applications in partnership with the managers (information consumers) showing their most critical data up through the close of business the day before. Leaders can quickly assess their safety scores, quality, and productivity rates, as well as any other information that is currently on their radar.

In five years, those applications will probably look like the dusty relics of a bygone age because everyone will get information delivered via Google glasses or whatever the Next Big Thing happens to be. Delivery modes may be an exciting thing to talk about, but delivery is not the issue. Creating a common and easily accessible library of the data already collected and asking the right questions—those are the real hurdles.

There is one more bit of advice that Brian would offer and Iodice touched on earlier: conduct an early self-assessment of your organization's technological or business intelligence maturity. This will help uncover looming pitfalls and blind alleys you had not considered.

Iodice and Salem Health used a private company's survey and assessment tools to gauge their maturity. Smaller organizations or teams just beginning the process may want to look to the Gartner model.[68] This widely used five-step model for IT maturity, as well as Gartner's four elements of predictive analytics, will be useful reading material for any leaders asking the essential first questions such as, *"Where are we now?"* and *"Are we ready for this?"*

All of this preparation is necessary because there are many forces aligned against the continuing success of a transition from data for reporting to data for improvement. And just as clear-eyed self-assessment of an organization's readiness for CBI is necessary, so is an assessment of the systemic barriers to the other elements of the lean transformation. The next chapter is a survey of barriers faced by healthcare organizations that choose the high road of the lean transformation. This is not a complaint; it is a call for some very specific changes.

---

68. http://www.gartner.com

10

Barriers
to the Work

Barriers are like enemies. We need to know them—what they look like and where they hide—in order to successfully navigate the trouble they cause. And some of those barriers are hidden behind pretty good camouflage.

Numerous obstacles to a lean transformation come from within an organization, many of which have been described in previous chapters. But the most difficult barriers may be lurking outside of healthcare. The three biggest barriers are medical education programs that churn out heroic individuals instead of team players, the lack of publicly available outcomes data for quality and cost, and perverse payment incentives. To be fair, most of these barriers are in direct response to the way doctors traditionally practiced medicine.

Physicians said that doctors should be solely in control of patient care and that doctors know best. Medical schools have been churning out autocratic, heroically minded physicians ever since. Physicians have not collected data on patient outcomes and have entered contracts with insurers to keep secret all payment information. So the public is largely blindfolded while making healthcare choices. The medical profession clings to a system in which providers are paid for work piecemeal and bill separately for each instance of service. So we have a system that pays for procedures instead of for health.

These arrangements are now outdated and counterproductive, especially for lean systems that have invested significant resources to improve patient care. In lean health systems, we have to spend time retraining physicians to see waste and potential for harm. We work hard to get patients into and out of treatment faster—reducing waiting times, creating shorter hospital stays—and therefore get paid less.

For instance, an improvement team in ThedaCare proved that by changing a few practices, they could drastically cut down on the amount of time that premature newborn babies spent in the neonatal ICU. That meant fewer billable days for ThedaCare's expensive NICU, even though the fixed costs of that expensive unit remained in place. So the reward for bringing less traumatized babies into the world was lower revenue. ThedaCare still made the changes because it was the right thing to do, but the incentives were running in the wrong direction.

Together, we need to pressure academia, the Centers for Medicare and Medicaid Services (CMS), and private insurers to correct their incentives and align with a lean system that puts the patient first and is always working toward better quality at lower cost. Many of us in lean healthcare are active in medical school governance, professional organizations, and government advisory groups. We need to use those positions to call for action. Specifically, we need payment reform, transparency of cost and quality data, and medical school and residency training that emphasizes teamwork and scientific problem solving.

Fortunately, there are people within academia, the government, and insurance companies that are helping push toward some of our goals. Let's check in with universities first.

"At every level of medical education there is a growing recognition that physicians are trained in scientific problem solving, but only as applied to medical problems. They are not trained to apply that same scientific method to problems in quality or safety improvement, resource stewardship, or systems-based practice," says John E. Billi, MD, professor of Internal Medicine, Learning Health Sciences, and Health Management and Policy and associate vice president for medical affairs at the University of Michigan. "The tide is starting to turn on that."

Dr. Billi is an optimist and an influential advocate for change. It is, however, a powerful tide that he faces. Medical education has a long history of being based in an apprenticeship model, in which the student learns his art from a great master and bases his career on those methods. This style of education was immortalized in the Hippocratic oath[69] and is still the modus operandi in most schools, particularly in training for the specialties. This apprenticeship model was fine for making violins in the fourteenth century or for teaching a trade that has stable, unchanging techniques.

For the rapidly changing world of medicine and healthcare, however, physicians, nurses, and other health professionals need to learn how to constantly evaluate their practice and the systems that support it. Instead of being focused only on individual roles and the methods they learned in school, they need to learn to be part of the whole team that delivers healthcare. As chief diagnostician, the doctor has an important role to play in directing team activities. But he or she alone does not deliver all the care a patient needs, and so, when thinking

---

69. The full text of the Hippocratic oath is in the appendix, figure 9.

about patient care, doctors need to learn to think well beyond their own actions.

Everyone on the care team, including the physician, must learn to rely on investigation and evidence when making decisions about the process of care. This means using not only the results of published scientific studies but also the results of investigations of the causes and countermeasures for problems in care delivery. Everyone needs to learn how to create standard work, use scientific thinking to address problems, and create processes that are for the benefit of the patient and the caregivers. Once again, this is a case where the right mind-set needs to be in place before anyone can tap the skill set and tool set. And this is where the curriculum needs an update.

Dr. Billi would have me underline the fact that medical education has changed much in the past 20 years to place more emphasis on basic science and hands-on training. That is certainly true. But schools are still producing physicians that are taught to act independently, instead of learning to be members of a team that provides care based on scientific thinking and problem solving. Dr. Billi is working on that.

"We have, for a century or more, actually taught students scientific problem solving. We call it Performing a History and Physical. We taught them A3 thinking, just under a different name," Dr. Billi says. "For example, we would never let a student diagnose a patient without examining the patient; that's just scientific problem solving. What we failed to do is teach the students that they were learning one specific application of a generalizable process that they could apply to all other problems they have—whether that is surgical site infections, an overflowing ED, or backups in the OR."

To begin correcting that oversight, Dr. Billi has helped install an elective in the second year of medical school called "How You and Your Team

Can Deliver Better Health Care: Applying Lean Thinking." This is an intensive first look into how lean works in healthcare, with students learning core concepts such as types of waste and standard work during a simulation of a night in the emergency department. They also participate in a gemba walk, follow nurses on an inpatient floor, and learn how to work through problems with a team using an A3.

During their fourth year, students can take the more intensive "Physicians as Leaders and Problem Solvers." In this full-time elective, students select a real problem, clinical or process based, and, over the course of four weeks, work through an A3 to find and document the root cause of the problem and propose countermeasures. Students also shadow University of Michigan Health System physician leaders, sit with them in administrative meetings, and spend time at the site of the problem that is their focus. They get real-world experience in solving the problems of a modern health system using the scientific process, Dr. Billi says.

Still, too few students are taught how to look for root causes and work in teams. Dr. Billi estimates that only 10%–20% of Michigan students leave with training in lean healthcare. Outside of Michigan, the outlook is grimmer. Johns Hopkins and the University of Washington both have some lean training. But there are 141 medical schools in the United States and less than a handful offer training in lean thinking or other problem-solving models.

Convincing one school at a time to develop expertise and offer lean training would take a very long time. What we need to do is convince the Liaison Committee on Medical Education, the medical school accreditation board, which has significant power over every school's curriculum, of the need to include lean thinking in the core studies of every student. As Dr. Billi knows, however, there is a long line of candidates hoping to add to the list of what medical students need to learn.

"As the biomedical knowledge base has mushroomed over the last two decades, the faculty who manage the med school curriculum have felt pressure to cram more and more of this information into the two-year basic science slot. It's like they need to get a bigger plunger," Dr. Billi says. "But you don't learn lean in a classroom; you learn it in the workplace, trying to solve real practice problems."

There is an experiment in progress that is worth watching. Since 2009, the Association of American Medical Colleges (AAMC) has sponsored Integrating Quality, an active interest group for medical schools engaged in teaching quality improvement in the clinical setting.[70] Schools share their experience in teaching and creating quality improvements in annual meetings and webinars. The American Medical Association (AMA) has sponsored 11 medical schools to revise their curricula to focus more on the skills needed for practice in the twenty-first century. This AMA program, Accelerating Change in Medical Education, fosters "redesigning medical school to facilitate improvement in care delivery and stewardship of our nation's resources."[71] The University of Michigan Medical School received one of the AMA grants and launched a wide-scale redesign of the curriculum.

For a while, Dr. Billi says, the leaders of the curricular reform discussed making a separate branch of study for *that lean stuff.*

"We convinced them, however, that lean concepts are so core to the practice of medicine in the twenty-first century that no physician can be without it," Dr. Billi says. "I see forces aligning themselves and pushing in the same direction. But there is enormous inertia, too. Medical education is an enormously complex value stream."

---

70.   https://www.aamc.org/initiatives/quality/

71.   http://www.ama-assn.org/ama/pub/about-ama/strategic-focus/accelerating-change-in-medical-education.page

Ideas on how to change the curriculum are still fairly fluid. There are strong opinions pressing on medical education from many sides. In order to start getting newly graduated physicians and nurses who are ready to solve problems and know PDSA thinking and how to work through an A3, we need to be part of the conversation about medical education. Your voices must be heard. Otherwise, we in lean healthcare will continue to spend resources retraining new medical school graduates out of the bad habits they spend years acquiring.

Another barrier to system transformation is payment; healthcare providers need to speak up about how they are paid. For too long, physicians have relied on the overly simplistic fee-for-service scheme, which worked very well for generations of country doctors and small practitioners who wrote a simple bill for the work they did. They saw patients; they treated patients; they got paid. Then the world sped up. The more patients that providers could see in a day—the more specialized surgeries performed, the more MRIs read—the more money people made. Nonprofit community hospitals were pushed by the financial realities of fee-for-service medicine to generate more medical interventions in order to maintain their financial health.

I know that the majority of providers never think about money when looking at a patient. They think about how to make that patient better. Still, the system of incentives is upside down. Fee for service has been one of the direct causes of spiraling healthcare costs that have been bankrupting families and companies and threatening to do the same to the entire country for more than 20 years.

Fee for service has not just failed to check runaway cost inflation but also created an expectation of more and more healthcare. Meanwhile, studies have proved that more healthcare does not make for a healthier population.

Since the early 1990s, the Dartmouth Atlas Project has been studying and publishing reports about healthcare utilization, clinical practices, and variations in patient care across the United States. Using data from Medicare and funded by the National Institutes of Health and grants from several independent foundations, research teams at Dartmouth University have discovered that huge variations exist in the way that medicine is practiced and healthcare delivered across the country.

In some states, Medicare pays out more than twice as much for patient care in one town as it does for another nearby. Moreover, the high variation in healthcare costs is not caused by price disparity. In pockets throughout the country, Medicare pays double because patients are getting a lot more "care." On the Dartmouth Atlas website, editors explain:

Simply put, in regions where there are more hospital beds per capita, patients will be more likely to be admitted to the hospital. In regions where there are more intensive care unit beds, more patients will be cared for in the ICU. More specialists will result in more visits to specialists. And the more CT scanners are available, the more CT scans patients will receive. The Dartmouth Atlas has consistently demonstrated these relationships.

In regions where there are relatively fewer medical resources, patients get less care; however, there is no evidence that these patients are worse off than their counterparts in high-resourced, high-spending regions. Patients do not experience improved survival or better quality of life if they live in regions with more care. In fact, the care they receive appears to be worse.[72]

Fee for service creates incentives to keep our hospitals filled and our patients coming back on a repeat loop. I do not believe that providers

---

72. "Key Issues: Supply-Sensitive Care." Accessed December 2, 2014. http://www.dartmouthatlas. org/keyissues/issue.aspx?con=2937

do this intentionally. But when there is no incentive not to, it just becomes a comfortable groove people fall into. When I was practicing, I used to imagine our frail elderly population traveling back and forth between hospitals and clinics on snowy highways on an unending trek to fix one discrete issue after another, and I felt terrible. More medicine is not better medicine.

So how much is enough? Do our patients really need to come into the clinic every month or quarter? In what situations are five heart stents better than four? When is precisely the best time for a hip replacement? We do not have scientific studies to answer every question. I am not sure that science *can* answer every question. So, we need to do a better job of setting priorities in the way we pay for healthcare and a system that produces better outcomes overall.

For instance, we know from Medicare data studies that medication reconciliation errors are the greatest source of patient harm. Following several experiments at ThedaCare and other health systems, we know that personal time with a trained pharmacist or pharmacy technician helps to eliminate these errors. Every healthcare organization ought to hire an army of pharmacists to coordinate with physicians and then visit every patient upon release from the hospital and to revisit periodically with patients battling chronic disease. They would meet in the patient's home to discuss medications, answer questions, and ensure that the patient was getting prescriptions filled and remembering to take the right doses. But health systems do not get paid for coordinating that kind of care. Private insurers and public programs such as Medicare pay only for fixing issues that should have been prevented in the first place.

Moving away from fee for service and instead pursuing a payment structure that will emphasize health over medical procedures will better serve patients and health systems alike. Risk-adjusted global payments are the most promising way to do this.

Currently in consideration for Medicare trials, risk-adjusted global payments offer per-month, per-patient payments to a health system to care for a person in sickness and in health. The payment amount is based on the patient's health risks: disease, chronic conditions, age, and other factors.

This is not the Health Maintenance Organization (HMO) model of the 1980s, where insurers were deciding what therapies would and would not be covered and thereby inserting themselves into clinical decisions. With risk-adjusted global payments, the health system or clinic accepts the risk along with the payment and makes the care decisions. Instead of a far-away bureaucrat, caregivers have the final call. (This will encourage those caregivers to remove waste and avoid costs such as avoidable hospitalizations.)

With risk-adjusted global payments, health systems have a strong incentive to keep people healthy. Instead of advertising the latest MRI or robotic surgery, the system must emphasize preventive care, patient safety, error reduction, and quality care for people just released from the hospital. Because getting it right the first time costs less money—a lot less money—and less pain for the patient.

With global payments, health systems will succeed or fail on quality of care and waste reduction. Hospitals and clinics that can improve productivity, reduce errors, and treat chronic conditions before people are in crisis will find money left over. The money health systems make, in other words, will be found in the margins.

Consider this, however: in Medicare's initial investigations into a payment mechanism that represented a step toward paying for value, 40% of the participating organizations dropped out after the second year, largely because they could not make the necessary improvement and so could not make it work financially. Following the second year of the Pioneer Accountable Care Organization (ACO) Model and Medicare Shared Savings Program in 2014, some of the organizations even owed the government money due to their inability to produce promised savings.[73]

The Bellin-ThedaCare Healthcare Partners ACO, on the other hand, started with one of the lowest baseline costs of the cohort of providers in this experiment and still managed to deliver promised savings to Medicare—as well as the highest-recorded quality rankings among more than 350 ACOs in the country.

This has highlighted an important reality: every health system must have some kind of organized, effective improvement process in place in order to be successful with risk-adjusted global payments. In the future, income will be dependent on cost reductions and quality improvements. An organization might choose not to follow a lean path, but all health systems will need to find an organizing principle to drive improvements. The 13 health systems—out of the original 32—that dropped out of Medicare's Shared Savings Program after the second year proved that.

We need to make the full switch to global payments quickly because fee for service does not work alongside a global payment system. If one part of your organization makes money on the old heads–in–beds model, which actually hurts your financial position with risk-adjusted global payment programs, the system is not sustainable. For instance, the Bellin-ThedaCare ACO used a systematically redesigned process for managing chronically ill patients and prevented about 500 Medicare admissions

---

73. The Shared Savings program was, unfortunately, still based in a fee-for-service world. In this model, Medicare noted how much it spent on healthcare for a population of patients in a particular health system or ACO in the previous year. Then Medicare adjusted the number for risk and made a deal with the ACO that, if it could lower that risk-adjusted per-patient cost by 2%, the ACO and Medicare would share the savings. But the health systems were still using fee for service with the upside-down incentives. The Shared Savings bonus often could not compete with the extra revenue from unimproved care.

in 2012. So Medicare saved money, while Bellin-ThedaCare ACO facilities' fixed costs, such as staff, equipment, and utilities, still accrued. ThedaCare's revenue fell by 0.7% during the first six months of that year. At ThedaCare, executives believe that at least 50% of patients need to be in global payments for the whole delivery system to fundamentally change processes. If more than half the patients are still being charged fee for service, the volume-of-care incentive will still be stronger than the value-of-care incentive.

While I believe that a risk-adjusted global payment system is our best hope for sustainable healthcare in the future, I am very aware that there are kinks to work out. If a patient wants to get a new knee outside of his or her own ACO network, how will the origin ACO be assured it is not liable for outsized bills? How will consumers pick between competing ACOs?

One current barrier to any system based even partially on market forces and consumer choice, such as risk-adjusted global payments, is the fact that consumers are asked to make choices without knowing the quality records and real costs of competing health systems. Without reliable data, they are blindfolded. Private systems—both insurers and providers—protect their information zealously; Medicare releases data only for specific studies, such as the Dartmouth Atlas studies.

There is no assumption that the public has a right to accurate, reliable quality and cost data in order to make informed choices. Yet, consumers must have these facts in order to make good decisions. Consumers should be able to find good information on clinical outcomes for hospitals, clinics, and individual physicians before we decide where to have a baby, get a new hip, or have a troublesome cough examined.

How do we get there? That question became my preoccupation. When I retired as CEO of ThedaCare in 2008, I became more involved in creating a Wisconsin statewide initiative to have all doctors and hospitals publicly reveal quality and cost data. The hope was that health systems and doctors who were doing the right thing would gain larger market share once consumers saw they had higher-quality outcomes and lower costs.[74] This could correct at least some of the inequities of fee for service.

The Wisconsin Health Information Organization now collects insurance claims from all physicians and hospitals in the state and creates reports that allow health systems to track how well they are doing against others. It is one of the most comprehensive all-claims databases in the country. Separately, a group of providers and health systems such as ThedaCare and Bellin also created the Wisconsin Collaborative for Healthcare Quality to publicly report our clinical performance data. Membership is voluntary, and about 65% of physicians in the state now belong.

The two initiatives are, admittedly, imperfect solutions. The data and reports produced by the all-claims database had just begun to be reported to the public in 2014, and reaction is yet unknown. Will consumers make informed choices using the data? And from the Collaborative, patients get the information that only 65% of doctors and health systems are willing to share. It is only the beginning of a solution, but we are working toward the goal of transparency.

To get to transparency, the data must be relevant. For data to be relevant, they must be complete and comparable. Consumers need to compare all apples to all apples. This will require a more unified effort at the national level.

I believe this future of risk-adjusted global payments and data transparency is coming at us fast because it is necessary and every

---

74. This effort and the outcomes are detailed in my book *Potent Medicine: The Collaborative Cure for Healthcare* (ThedaCare Center for Healthcare Value: 2012)

healthcare provider needs to be prepared. Most are not. To get there, better healthcare delivery systems are needed. And every healthcare organization needs an improvement process that drives toward problem solving, waste reduction, and getting it right the first time. Lean healthcare is not the only way to get there; it is simply the best, most comprehensive methodology to transform an organization into a problem-solving culture that I have encountered.

For that reason, let's return to the step-by-step implementation of a system-wide lean initiative. When you see all the steps laid down, one after another, it is easier to imagine the whole organism working in harmony.

11

Taking
the First Step

If a lean health system can be equated with the human body—complex, multifunctional, interconnected—then what you have read about so far in this book has been the skeleton. As with any skeleton, it must carry the weight of a body and allow for movement, so this structure is critically important.

Since leaving ThedaCare in 2008, I have been allowed to examine many health systems undergoing lean transformations and so feel confident that this skeleton of a lean transformation has all the right pieces in place. In this final chapter let's move through all the steps in order to see the dynamic interactions that will occur.

Self-assessing your leadership team's readiness for change is a step that many organizations think they can skip. But remember the admonition, "Physician, know thyself." This drive toward operational excellence will place great stress on your senior team. Before setting out, it is crucial to stop and carefully inspect the vehicle to make sure it is ready. Know your team's strengths and weaknesses; prepare everyone to work together far more closely than they have in the past.

If your senior meetings are typically marked by turf battles and seething resentment, this step may take longer than anticipated. A team that is at war with itself cannot create positive change for others. More than once I have seen promising transformation efforts explode due to personality conflicts and a lack of unified vision in the C-suite.

Most self-assessments have some element of group therapy. Senior leaders have a tendency to believe they are doing everything right. After all, nobody gets to the C-suite by chance alone. Now these executives will be asked to fundamentally change the way they lead—to become more collaborative, to learn how to follow standard work, to become focused on patients instead of their own silos, and to be driven by metrics. This is where you need the objectivity of data.

Getting data to help guide leaders toward change is why you need HR and organizational development on board, facilitating 360-degree reviews and counseling senior leaders on their results. I have met few people who actually enjoy 360-degree reviews, but I know of no other way to collect real data over time that can be presented to leaders as they try to move the needle on personal and team development. These are tough conversations to have. With data to use as a guide, however, it can feel less personal and more productive.

This is also the point where leaders of HR and organizational development need to begin changes within their own departments to better support a lean organization. HR will need to deploy people out into the organization to work on teams and collaborate on new job definitions. In most companies, organizational development teams are dedicated to interventions after things go wrong, working with dysfunctional teams and leaders. Like HR, this team will be called on from the very beginning to work proactively instead of reactively, getting frontline teams and senior management ready for change. The organizational development team will need to create change management standard work—ready for testing, auditing, and improving—for frontline teams, as well.

The model cell should not be a surprise to anyone. People will have heard of the coming changes and will be very curious as to how the model cell works and what it looks like. Use this to your advantage. The model cell should be a teaching tool as much as it is an experiment in transforming value-creating processes.

The reason that the model cell moved to the front of the action plan[75] is that I have discovered that there is no greater power than hands-on learning. With the model cell, senior leaders must agree on and clearly state the real business problem they are trying to solve. Teams, which include executives and the CEO, must use lean tools such as A3s to address real problems that need immediate attention. Hands-on work is the way to hardwire principles and behaviors, such as scientific thinking and team-based problem solving, throughout the system.

While the model cell is in planning and early-building stages, organizational development should be preparing the staff and managers in the model-cell experiment area to work together as a team. In collaboration with HR and operations, people in organizational development need to be infusing new skills in the management team. Managers should all be learning how to build and follow standard work, create visual management, and mentor their direct reports. (The daily management system is not called for until step five, but organizations such as PAMF have found it very useful to include some elements of daily management from the first model cell.)

---

75. In my first book, *On the Mend,* I suggested that organizations first identify their crisis point in order to create a bias for action. After seeing dozens of transformations in action, I now believe that the inspiration and practical reality of a model cell is far more effective than the urgency of a burning platform.

The model cell has also proved a necessary early step because it provides a focus for everyone's arguments. Think about the experiences of Dr. Conroy at PAMF or Dr. MacKenzie at Lehigh Valley Health Network. Both physicians talked about standing in the model cell and showing their colleagues exactly how things would look and how they worked. Without the physical reality of a working cell, all they would have had was talk. It is enormously difficult, I find, to win people over to revolutionary change without being able to show the future being offered. The model cell is that future.

Values and principles need to be clear and settled. Most companies have a set of values that were written along with the mission statement. Principles, which are the stated methods to be used to achieve the values, will likely need to be written anew at the beginning of your transformation.

Lean principles can and should be learned while teams are building the model cell. These should be written in such a way as to serve as a reference point for all improvement work. Over time, the principles will guide the behavioral expectations for all.

I strongly recommend that any organization using lean thinking as an organizing methodology build its principles using the Shingo model. Respect every individual. Lead with humility. Seek perfection. Ensure quality at the source. Employ scientific thinking. Focus on process. Think systemically. Create constancy of purpose. Achieve transparency through visual management.

Each of these principles should be demonstrated in the model cell and taught in every new training course because these are the guides for every choice made.

The central improvement team is not just an incredibly useful group of facilitators who will teach and lead lean improvements. It is the future of your organization. The training and experience that are part of being on a central improvement team will help you build a new kind of manager—one who has led improvement teams throughout the organization and understands the necessity of scientific problem solving.

From the very beginning, assign your brightest stars to this team. I have seen organizations park underperforming or tolerable staff members on a central improvement team and it always backfires. This team roster tells the rest of the organization how highly you value your improvement program. By rotating the most valuable players through this team, you clearly signal that operations excellence is your main focus.

Those who do well on the central improvement team should also be assured of a better position upon leaving the team. I have long advocated a two-year rotation on a central improvement team for all future leaders as part of an advancement plan. A manager might join the team knowing that she would be a director after two years, and a director would know that his next job would be as a vice president. In this way, acquiring a deep knowledge of lean healthcare thinking and methods should be seen as the path to advancement.

I have also seen a few organizations offer one-year or 18-month rotations in the lean office, after which the leader returns to his or her previous job. This also seems to work well, as long as the leader is not expected to fulfill any part of his previous job while on the central improvement team. Using either scheme, it should be clear to everyone that one day soon, the CEO will be a former central improvement team member.

Now that your organization will be moving people into different jobs more frequently, HR will need to get involved in establishing rules for how people get transferred. With a no-layoff-due-to-improvement policy in place—a must-have for every lean organization—HR will also need to establish job pools and retraining programs for people who are made redundant through productivity improvements.

Finance gets into the action here, as well. As soon as improvement teams start reporting on how much money was saved, how many investments were avoided, and how many FTEs were not hired, some people will become very interested in debating about the return on investment. Many people have experiences like that of Helen Macfie at MemorialCare in Southern California, where worrying over ROI began driving a wedge between finance and operations. Work on coming to a clear and early understanding between finance and the central improvement team about ROI and how to calculate savings from improvement and whether such calculations are actually necessary.

The daily management system is so crucial to the health of an improvement initiative that some organizations have begun their lean journeys here. Certainly, elements of a daily management system such as leadership standard work can and should be launched with the model cell. From what I have seen, however, actually changing your entire management structure along with roles and responsibilities requires a more robust lean structure, which an organization should be acquiring by this point, after the model cell and central improvement teams are in place.

When everyone knows that a major transformation is inevitable, personal change in leadership style will seem a bit more palatable. Moving from management by objectives to management by process in this environment may even feel welcome. The key here is to clearly state the new roles being played by each level of management and the competencies that everyone will need to acquire.

Senior management will need to absorb—and reflexively use—A3 thinking. Every senior leader will need to learn to be comfortable and productive at gemba, use visual management, create and stick to True North metrics, and focus on the most critical projects with strategy deployment. It is a steep learning curve for the C-suite.

Middle managers will also learn how to be useful at gemba, create and use visual management tools, and support improvement projects that support True North metrics. Additionally, they will conduct daily status-sheet meetings with their clinical leads and huddles with full teams to reveal defects and opportunities for improvement. Middle managers will begin collaborating more closely with members of support services such as HR, finance, and business intelligence in monthly scorecard meetings. They will audit standard work, mentor frontline clinical leaders, and identify and address problems using PDSA cycles. Most importantly, they will learn to teach and mentor their clinical leads—spotting and nurturing tomorrow's leaders.

Supervisors are responsible in most organizations for whatever tasks are assigned ad hoc by their managers. For many, this is a scut-work position. In a daily management system, however, supervisors have important jobs that feed frontline information to the entire system. Supervisors train frontline workers in PDSA thinking and make sure that problems are identified and addressed by people on the front line.

The clinical business intelligence team will need to be deeply involved in this work, as well, as they learn to support the new information needs of leaders at every level.

Spreading the work from the model cell to the rest of the organization is not a copy-and-paste operation. Think of it as copy/improve because every iteration of the model cell should bear the fingerprints of the people who work in that new cell and should offer up improvement ideas on the original to share with the rest of the organization.

To do this right, the model cell must have a robust process, well documented with standard work for each actor. Remember: there can be no improvement without standard work in place.

Standard work, however, should not be rigid. At PAMF, for instance, the model-cell standard work was for all physicians to sit with medical assistants to facilitate easy communication about every aspect of the day. The standards did not specify what kind of desk should be used, or the precise distance between desks, or what time physician-assistant conversations took place.

Organizations that try to enforce a copy/paste approach risk strangling any sense of innovation. And, from what I have seen, they have a much harder time implementing the ideas of the model cell in new areas. Keep in mind that people, in general, do not like to be told what to do. If they are presented with successful experiments, however, and offered useful templates, they will naturally look for ways to improve and personalize the model.

Think of James Hereford running into resistance as he told new sites at Group Health in Seattle that they would be getting this terrific new process. When he moved to PAMF in the Bay Area, he took a more collaborative approach. To the leadership in each clinic, he and his team presented findings from the model cell and then basically said, "Here is our best thinking to date on how to make a better clinic. Does it make sense for you? If not, how can you do better?"

The spread of the model-cell work at PAMF was notable for its speed and ease. It was the kind of new-process rollout that any organization would envy.

Planning and building the model cell are really where **support services such as finance, HR, organizational development, and business intelligence** should learn and adjust to their new roles in the larger system. Every department should be thinking about how it fits into and supports the model cell, not the other way around.

Often, this calls for a major redesign of the way these departments operate. HR will need to be proactively involved in the improvement projects that might make people redundant, for instance, in order to ease their transition to other jobs. Finance will need to redeploy its auditors away from building budgets to advising managers on how to think about and improve the finances of their areas. And computer data analysts will need to work more closely with managers and other leaders, learning about the questions they really need answered.

People in support services will sometimes need to relearn their priorities. They are not accountants or data farmers or even employees of HR. Everyone is there to work for the patient. Support staff is additionally responsible to workers at the front line, where value is being created.

In systems that have undergone this transformation, I have seen that the daily management system, including the redefinition of job roles and responsibilities, is the biggest issue for HR. For financial analysts, shifting focus away from departmental budgets and toward optimizing patient care is the major hurdle. And for a computer analyst, working with people to find out what information they really need and then building the systems to provide it is a very big pivot.

The changes are big and challenging, but they are entirely worthwhile. I have spoken with many auditors, analysts, and clerks who are far happier now that they have been liberated from their desks in back offices. Working alongside frontline caregivers, they are more engaged in the primary work of the health system: helping people.

Of course, it is not just support services that are bound for wrenching change. Think about taking a survey of all people in your organization to ask about the central focus of their job. Who are they there to serve?

A substantial percentage would say they are paid to support physicians, to run machines, to clean floors, or to assist nurses. It is the wrong answer.

The purpose of this transformation is to create a culture of care centered on the patient's well-being. This involves the relentless pursuit of operational excellence, breaking down silos that keep us focused within our departments, and continuous improvement.

I hope that we—not just me and ThedaCare but also all of the organizations surveyed in this book and the people who have worked so hard to transform them—have pushed you into the camp of believers. We share these stories because we know that the principles of lean thinking work in healthcare. We know that our industry needs to change radically to meet the coming challenges, and we have discovered the way to do it, while making our people more engaged and focused on patient care.

This journey, like all of them, starts with the first step forward. Join us.

Acknowledgments

My deepest appreciation is reserved for my wife, Susan, and her patience over the past year as my focus shifted so completely onto this book. I would also thank my son, Ted, for long conversations and helping me to think in new ways about old problems.

Thank you to Emily Adams, for her dexterity with words and her ability to make stories come alive; to Jim Womack for his red pen and his unswerving guidance on message clarity; and to Devon Ritter for her patience and attention to detail.

To Michael Erikson and Michael Conroy, MD, at Palo Alto Medical Foundation; James Hereford at Stanford Hospital and Clinics; Chris Kita and Richard MacKenzie, MD, at Lehigh Valley Health Network; Rachelle Schultz at Winona Health; Mary Kingston at Little Company of Mary Medical Center; and Cara Bailey, Lynn Martin, MD, Mark Reed, MD, and Thomas Hansen, MD, at Seattle Children's Hospital, thank you for your generosity of time in telling your stories. To Jack Billi, MD, at the University of Michigan Medical School; Kathryn Correia and Didier Rabino at HealthEast; Brian McGinnis, Shana Herzfeldt, Roger Gerard, Kathy Franklin, and Brian Burmeister at ThedaCare and Matt Furlan, now at Sutter Health; the entire CBI team at Salem Health; Jeff Mainland at SickKids in Toronto; Helen Macfie at MemorialCare Health System; and all the teams that support these leaders and do the real work, you have my sincerest appreciation.

Thank you to Kim Barnas, who helped us see what good looks like for lean management.

To all my team at the ThedaCare Center for Healthcare Value for their continued great work and specifically to Steven Bollinger, director of product development, and Helen Zak, president and COO, thank you for keeping us supported. Thank you to Brian Veara of the Clinical

Business Intelligence Network for the precision of his contributions and to Steve Player of the Beyond Budgeting Roundtable for working over the holidays to make sure we got the story straight. And to my many mentors including Paul O'Neill, George Koenigsaecker, Orry Fiume, John Shook, Walt Rugland, Maureen Bisognano, Don Berwick, Dan Ariens, Leonard Berry, and Jose Bustillo, my profound appreciation. I have learned so much from them and many others and am very grateful for that.

To Healthcare Value Network leader Larry Antonucci, who carefully read an early draft, as well as Patrick Decoster in Belgium and Alex Munter in Ontario, Canada, thank you for your time and careful attention. And to our other Network CEOs who are transforming their own organizations, thank you for the daily inspiration.

Finally, my deep appreciation to the board members of the ThedaCare Center for Healthcare Value who have helped me on many occasions and continue to provide terrific counsel as we move the industry closer to operational excellence using lean.

Part III

Appendix

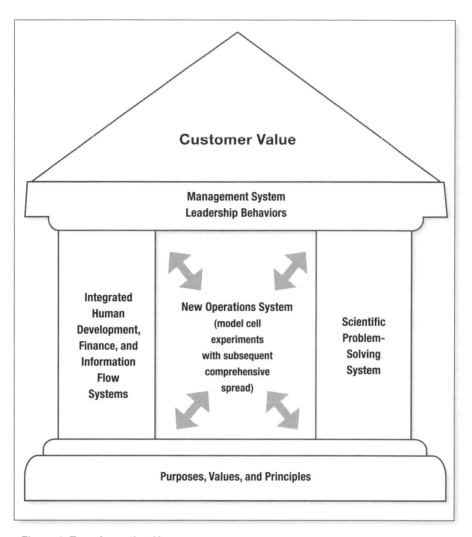

Figure 1. Transformation House

This house represents the overall elements of a lean healthcare transformation.

The foundation is created from values and principles defined by leaders guiding the transformation. New operations systems, including the model cell and the subsequent spread of that work, are built on this foundation and guided by the management system and better leadership behaviors. The two pillars giving strength and stability to the house are the newly integrated support services and scientific problem solving.

Each element of this house represents a redesign of the way that healthcare is delivered. When support services such as human resources, finance, and information (or business intelligence) are integrated, they cease operating as separate silos and become focused on the needs of patients and on supporting frontline workers. Instead of performance reviews, budgets, and data reports, support services all become invested in helping caregivers solve problems using the scientific method. Key issues include developing future leaders, moving from budgets to forecasting, and focusing on improvement opportunities rather than retrospective analysis. These pillars make a lean transformation strong, while a redesigned daily management system that enables everyone to solve the right problems today provides structure for all improvement efforts.

The goal of all this activity is to create customer value. We define value as constantly delivering higher-quality, lower-cost care that continuously improves over time. Achieving this goal requires more than a few handy fixes. This is the redesign required by the future of healthcare.

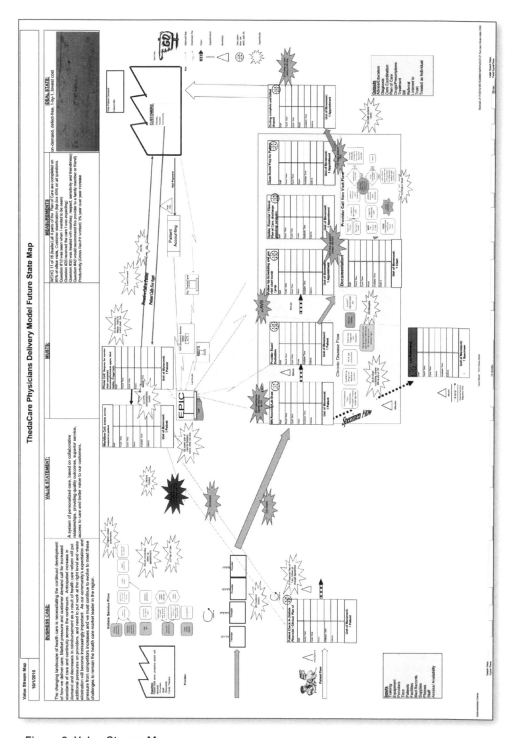

Figure 2. Value Stream Map

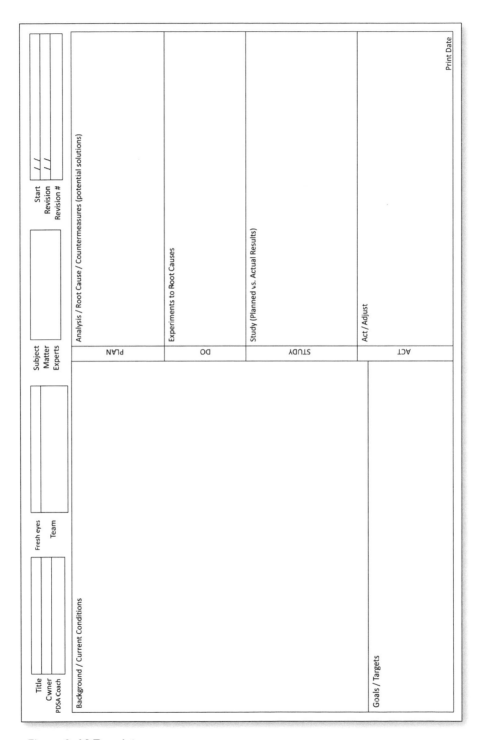

Figure 3. A3 Template

THE FIVE WHYS

Determining value and waste is no simple task. Ingrained habits take on the patina of having value, simply because the actions are so often repeated. Labeling a habit as waste usually means busting a few paradigms, and for that, special tools are required. A simple tool is to exercise curiousity and, for every problem, ask "why." Then ask "why" four times more.

For example, let's examine why a patient with an apparent ST segment elevated myocardial infarction, or STEMI, is waiting in the emergency room instead of receiving a life-saving balloon angioplasty.

1. Why the wait? Because the patient needs a cardiology consult.

2. Why the consult? Because the cardiologists say they must be the ones to diagnose a STEMI event.

3. Why cardiologists? Because the cardiologists do not trust the emergency doctors to accurately diagnose a STEMI.

4. Why the distrust? Because emergency doctors have not been specifically trained to recognize a STEMI event.

5. Why? There is no standardized process to diagnose a STEMI event.

The countermeasure: develop a standardized process by which anyone could recognize and accurately diagnose a STEMI event. Write it out in clear instructions and post it for all to see.

Figure 4. The Five Whys

PROMISES BEHAVIOR GUIDE

PUT THE CUSTOMER FIRST:

- We bring to our work respect and positive attitudes.
- We listen to our customers and each other with compassion.
- We speak in clear, friendly language so that everyone understands.
- We focus on mind/body/spirit, journeying with the patient.
- We involve the patients in their care.
- We follow through on promises we make, advocate for the patient, and keep the patient safe.
- We anticipate customer needs, with smooth transitions from shift to shift and from one part of ThedaCare to another.

BE COURAGEOUS:

- Do what's right. Never ignore things that are wrong.
- Set challenging targets. Challenge the status quo, and be open to change.
- Be willing to lead.
- Say what we see, with honesty/kindness.
- Call out mistakes and bad behavior.
- Work through disagreements respectfully.
- Never hide from truth. Let evidence guide work.
- Support one another in challenging situations.

HAVE A THIRST FOR LEARNING:

- Be willing to be influenced (humility).
- Lead with questions (curiosity). Go and see!
- Seek out learning opportunities.
- Let someone know when things go wrong, and treat mistakes as learning.
- Seek out change that helps the patient. See the patient as a teacher.
- Take initiative to try new things. Improve something every day.
- Teach others what we know.

LOVE OUR WORK:

- Be a champion and show your passion.
- Respect the team and share the credit: "we" vs. "I."
- Offer a smile to others. See the good in everyone.
- Own our work. Turn complaints into solutions.
- Compassion (caring) to all.
- We never do harm and keep one another safe!
- Take pride in our work and in ThedaCare.
- Get to know the patients and the staff.
- See challenges as part of the fun.
- Celebrate! Appreciate others.

Figure 5. Promises Behavior Guide

CAREER TRANSITIONS FLOW

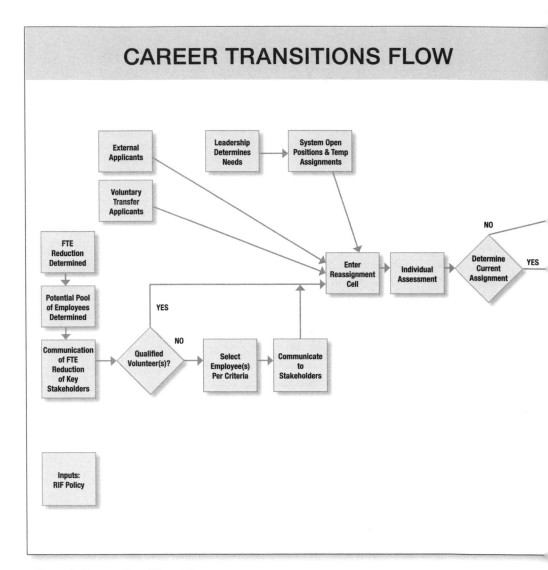

Figure 6. Career Transitions Flow

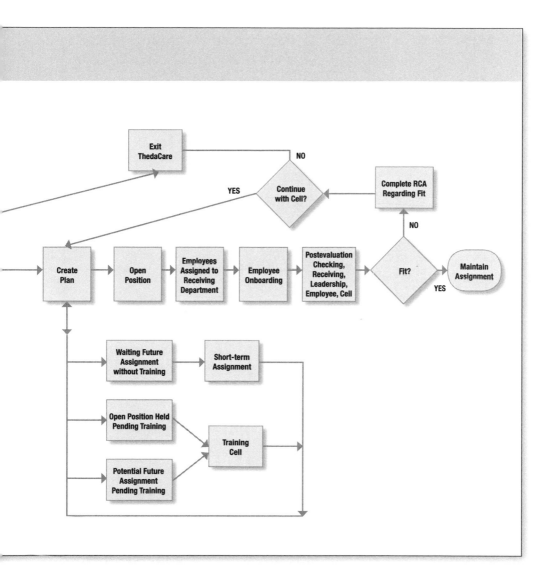

Figure 6. Career Transitions Flow *(continued)*

Succession Plan

Position	Incumbent	Date
Chief Executive Officer	Thomas N. Hansen, M.D.	4/10
Candidate	**Current Position**	**Timing**
John Jones	SVP for Corporate Services	3–5 years
Key Job Requirements	**Development Plans**	**Time Line**

EXPERIENCE --

Key Job Requirements	Development Plans	Time Line
• Experience leading a tertiary academic medical center.	• Has worked in large tertiary academic medical center. Needs experience with operations.	3–7 years
• Experience working with physicians and scientists in clinical, educational, and research environment.	• Through his current work with corporate services, he is gaining experience working with physicians and scientists.	3–5 years
• Experience supporting the structure, process, and policies of corporate governance.	• Needs more experience with governance. Will continue to have him present at board meetings and will look for appropriate board committee experience.	3–5 years
• Fund-raising experience.	• Needs much more experience with fund-raising and will be working with chief development officer to get that experience.	3 years
• Extensive experience with CPI—Toyota Lean Manufacturing.	• Has started CPI training and will go to Japan in December.	1–3 years

CAPABILITIES --

Key Job Requirements	Development Plans	Time Line
• Ability to articulate a vision.	• Already outstanding at articulating a vision, inspiring and leading change, and strategic thinking.	Now
• Ability to inspire and lead change.		
• A strategic thinker who can lead a strategic planning effort and implement the plan.		
• Ability to play strong external role—excellent relationship builder, effective in presenting to large groups, ability to fund-raise, and comfortable in a political realm.	• Needs to get out into community more to build strong external relationships. Already networking effectively in hospital community and needs to get involved in other areas of community relations. Has recently joined a not-for-profit board. Encourage him to join Rotary.	2–4 years
• Strong financial management expertise.	• He has strong financial management expertise and is an outstanding recruiter.	Done
• Effective at recruiting and developing top talent.		
• Excellent verbal and written communication skills with large and small audiences.	• He has excellent verbal and written communication skills with large and small audiences.	Done

QUALITIES AND SKILLS --

Key Job Requirements	Development Plans	Time Line
• A servant leader—an executive whose first priority is to serve an organization and its mission.	• His personal qualities and skills meet all of the criteria listed to the left.	Done
• Team-oriented approach that effectively promotes collaboration—a good coach and mentor.		
• Knows how to create a positive environment/culture to motivate and inspire people to achieve high performance and effectively manage conflict.		
• A style that is open to change and innovation, a commitment to continuous learning and self-improvement, a good sense of humor.		

Figure 7. Succession Plan

CEO Organization – SVP Level
Position Bench Strength

* = Emergency Situation

Position (incumbent)	Ready 0–12 months	Ready 1–2 years	Ready 3–5 years
CEO	1–2 candidates	1–2 candidates	2–4 candidates
President, Children's Hospital	1–2 candidates	1–2 candidates	2–4 candidates
President, Research Institute	1–2 candidates	1–2 candidates	2–4 candidates
SVP, Hospital Operations	1–2 candidates	1–2 candidates	2–4 candidates
SVP, Chief Nurse	1–2 candidates	1–2 candidates	2–4 candidates
President, Foundation	1–2 candidates	1–2 candidates	2–4 candidates
SVP, CIO	1–2 candidates	1–2 candidates	2–4 candidates
SVP, General Counsel	1–2 candidates	1–2 candidates	2–4 candidates
SVP, Medical Director	1–2 candidates	1–2 candidates	2–4 candidates
SVP, Chief Academic Office	1 candidate	JW-led search	UW-led search
SVP, Surgeon-in-Chief, President, CUMG	1 candidate	2–4 candidates	2–4 candidates
SVP, Strategic Planning	1 candidate	2–4 candidates	2–4 candidates
SVP, CFO	1 candidate	2–4 candidates	2–4 candidates
SVP, Shared Services	1 candidate	2–4 candidates	2–4 candidates
SVP, CPI	1 candidate	2–4 candidates	2–4 candidates

Figure 8. Position Bench Strength

HIPPOCRATIC OATH

I SWEAR TO FULFILL, TO THE BEST OF MY ABILITY AND JUDGMENT, THIS COVENANT:

I will respect the hard-won scientific gains of those physicians in whose steps I walk, and gladly share such knowledge as is mine with those who are to follow.

I will apply, for the benefit of the sick, all measures which are required, avoiding those twin traps of overtreatment and therapeutic nihilism.

I will remember that there is art to medicine as well as science, and that warmth, sympathy, and understanding may outweigh the surgeon's knife or the chemist's drug.

I will not be ashamed to say "I know not," nor will I fail to call in my colleagues when the skills of another are needed for a patient's recovery.

I will respect the privacy of my patients, for their problems are not disclosed to me that the world may know. Most especially must I tread with care in matters of life and death. If it is given me to save a life, all thanks. But it may also be within my power to take a life; this awesome responsibility must be faced with great humbleness and awareness of my own frailty. Above all, I must not play at God.

I will remember that I do not treat a fever chart, a cancerous growth, but a sick human being, whose illness may affect the person's family and economic stability. My responsibility includes these related problems, if I am to care adequately for the sick.

I will prevent disease whenever I can, for prevention is preferable to cure.

I will remember that I remain a member of society, with special obligations to all my fellow human beings, those sound of mind and body as well as the infirm.

If I do not violate this oath, may I enjoy life and art, respected while I live and remembered with affection thereafter. May I always act so as to preserve the finest traditions of my calling and may I long experience the joy of healing those who seek my help.

Figure 9. Hippocratic Oath

Bibliography, Further Reading

Barnas, Kim. *Beyond Heroes: A Lean Management System for Healthcare*. Appleton, WI: ThedaCare Center for Healthcare Value, 2014.

Cunningham, Jean E., and Orest J. Fiume. *Real Numbers: Management Accounting in a Lean Organization*. Durham, NC: Managing Times Press, 2003.

Deming, W. Edwards. *Out of the Crisis*. Cambridge, MA: MIT Press, 2000.

Dennis, Pascal. *Getting the Right Things Done: A Leader's Guide to Planning and Execution*. Cambridge, MA: Lean Enterprise Institute, 2006.

Koenigsaecker, George. *Leading the Lean Enterprise Transformation*. New York: Productivity Press, 2009.

Mann, David. *Creating a Lean Culture*. Boca Raton, FL: CRC Press, 2010.

Marquardt, Michael J. *Leading with Questions: How Leaders Find the Right Solutions by Knowing What to Ask*. San Francisco: Jossey-Bass, 2014.

Player, Steve, and Steve Morlidge. *Future Ready: How to Master Business Forecasting*. Hoboken, NJ: John Wiley & Sons, 2010.

Rother, Mike, and John Shook. *Learning to See: Value Stream Mapping to Add Value and Eliminate Muda*. Cambridge, MA: Lean Enterprise Institute, 1999.

Shook, John. *Managing to Learn*. Cambridge, MA: Lean Enterprise Institute, 2008.

Toussaint, John. "Essential Elements for the Success of the ACO Model." *Journal of the American Medical Association* 310, no. 13 (2013): 1341–1342.

Toussaint, John. "A Management, Leadership, and Board Road Map to Transforming Care for Patients." *Frontiers of Health Services Management* 29 (2014): 3.

Toussaint, John, and Roger A. Gerard. *On the Mend, Revolutionizing Healthcare to Save Lives and Transform the Industry.* Cambridge, MA: Lean Enterprise Institute, 2010.

Toussaint, John S., and Melissa Mannon. "Hospitals Are Finally Starting to Put Real-Time Data to Use." *Harvard Business Review* 2014. https://hbr.org/2014/11/hospitals-are-finally-starting-to-put-real-time-data-to-use.

Womack, James P., and Daniel T. Jones. *Lean Thinking: Banish Waste and Create Wealth in Your Corporation.* 2nd ed. Florence, MA: Free Press, 2003.

Publisher's Note

The publisher is profoundly grateful to these members of the Healthcare Value Network and other organizations for their leaders' willingness to share successes and failures in this book. Because a healthcare transformation has no end, we applaud the determination of the individuals within these organizations for the effort they demonstrate every day. Only through this relentless determination will we be able to provide a safe and sustainable healthcare system in North America.

Palo Alto Medical Foundation

Winona Health

ThedaCare

Salem Health

Lehigh Valley Health Network

SickKids

Seattle Children's

MemorialCare Health System

Providence Little Company of Mary

HealthEast

University of Michigan Health System

Index

Page numbers in *italic* indicate figures. An *n* after a page number indicates a footnote.

Endnote

This book was published by the ThedaCare Center for Healthcare Value. The Center was created in 2008 by the board of trustees of ThedaCare Inc. with the intention of transforming the healthcare industry to provide better value for patients. The Center offers education in lean healthcare and assists organizations that are implementing lean thinking.

Using the experiences of ThedaCare and other high-performing healthcare organizations, the Center creates and is constantly expanding its curriculum of books, videos, experiential learning opportunities, and peer-to-peer collaborative learning networks. Many resources are free. This book is just one offering for organizations seeking to align leadership practices with lean thinking. For more information, visit createvalue.org.

The Center also created and manages the **Healthcare Value Network** to facilitate collaboration in lean thinking. The Healthcare Value Network unites leaders who share a commitment to providing high-quality, cost-effective care through the application of lean concepts. Our members develop peer-to-peer relationships, share knowledge, conduct real-world experiments, and access the best resources to accelerate their organization's lean transformation. createvalue.org/networks/healthcare-value-network

The **Clinical Business Intelligence Network** unites healthcare leaders who are responsible for information content, flow, and access to support and accelerate their organization's journey toward becoming a high-value delivery system. Members develop peer-to-peer relationships; share knowledge; conduct real-world experiments; and access the best clinical analytics, business intelligence, and lean IT leaders in the industry. createvalue.org/networks/clinical-business-intelligence-network